# Story Play

## Bringing Books to Life in the Classroom

Muriel K. Rand

Creative Design by Catherine L. Rand

PRINCETON
SQUARE
PRESS

Published by Princeton Square Press
23 Ashford Drive Plainsboro, NJ 08536

ISBN-979-8-9873072-0-5

Dedicated to the teachers and administrators in Bridgeton, NJ Public Schools for co-creating these ideas with me and welcoming me into their classrooms:

Barbara Wilchensky, Director of Curriculum, Language Arts Literacy
Monica Poland, Principal, Dr. Geraldine O. Foster Early Childhood Center
Kelia Brown, Assistant Principal, Dr. Geraldine O. Foster Early Childhood Center
Kristi Schoppe, Assistant Principal, Quarter Mile Lane School

### *Teachers:*
Elyse Bittner
Tabitha Cassidy
Diana Cintron
Lauren Clark
Sandra Connor
Cherie Douglas
Lisa Duffield
Michele Evans
Tiffanie Miller
Stephanie Saul
Angela Surace
Nancy Wheaton

### *Master Teachers:*
Olga Carlson
Lisa Murphy
Denise Riley
Leah Taylor

# Contents

Introduction .................................................................................................. 1

Why Use Story Play? ....................................................................................... 3

    Story Play Research .................................................................................. 4

Planning for Story Play ................................................................................... 5

Managing Behaviors During Story Play ......................................................... 8

Props: Choosing and Making Materials .......................................................... 9

Original Stories and Story Play ..................................................................... 13

    Planning for Original Story Play ............................................................. 14

Extending Story Play ..................................................................................... 15

    Literacy Extensions ................................................................................. 15

    Story Play Thematic Units ...................................................................... 16

    Library Center Props ............................................................................... 19

    Dramatic Play Center .............................................................................. 21

    Art and Story Play .................................................................................. 22

    Writing and Story Play ........................................................................... 24

    Science and Engineering and Story Play ................................................. 27

The Teacher as a Play Partner ....................................................................... 31

Assessing Story Play ...................................................................................... 33

    Story Play Assessment Rubric ................................................................ 33

    Story Play and Common Core State Standards in Kindergarten ............. 36

Story Play Ideas ............................................................................................. 39

Abiyoyo by Pete Seeger ................................................................................. 40

Adventures of Gary and Harry: ..................................................................... 41

Brown Bear, Brown Bear by Bill Martin, Jr. ...................................................................... 42

Chicka Chicka Boom Boom by Bill Martin, Jr. and John Archambault ................................ 43

The Doorbell Rang by Pat Hutchins ................................................................................. 44

Gingerbread Man by Bonnie Dobkin .............................................................................. 45

Goldilocks and the Three Bears – Traditional ................................................................... 40

The Grouchy Ladybug by Eric Carle ............................................................................... 41

Henny Penny - Traditional .............................................................................................. 42

Hush! A Thai Lullaby by Minfong Ho ............................................................................. 49

The Icky Sticky Frog by Dawn Bentley ........................................................................... 50

The Little Mouse, The Red Ripe Strawberry, and the Big Hungry Bear by Don and Audrey
Wood ............................................................................................................................. 51

The Mixed-Up Chameleon by Eric Carle ......................................................................... 52

One Dog Canoe by Mary Casanova .................................................................................. 53

The Paper Bag Princess by Robert Munsch ....................................................................... 54

Pete the Cat and His Four Groovy Buttons by Eric Litwin .............................................. 55

Pete the Cat: I Love My White Shoes by Eric Litwin ...................................................... 50

There's An Alligator Under the Bed by Mercer Mayer ..................................................... 51

Three Billy Goats Gruff – Traditional .............................................................................. 52

The Three Little Pigs – Version by Bonnie Dobkin ......................................................... 53

Recommended Book List .................................................................................................. 60

Appendix A: Story Play Printables ................................................................................... 63

Appendix B: How We Do Story Play in Our Classroom ................................................... 80

References ........................................................................................................................ 87

# Introduction

Story play is a powerful strategy for engaging young children in books. Once the teacher has read a story aloud, the children take on the roles of the characters and reenact the story as part of the read aloud period. The story play experience provides the following advantages:

- Active engagement in the story
- Vocabulary development
- Identifying the main idea and details of the stories
- Understanding story elements and structure such as characters, plot episodes, conflict, resolution
- Developing confidence in speaking
- Self-regulation
- Joyful associations with literature

This book provides an overview of story play and many variations for using it in your classroom. Some teachers carry out story play once a month, others use it more frequently. There are many ways to extend story play into other activities during the day, and some teachers have children write their own original stories and then act them out.

Teachers who use story play say that their students are more involved, interested, and participate more than when they read the book alone. The students become excited for story time to begin!

Story play is a method of integrating a story book read aloud with socio-dramatic play activities. The process typically extends over a few days. The first day or two, the teacher reads a story to the class or small group and discusses the story elements: characters, setting, plot, solution, and focuses on target vocabulary words. The next day, the children choose character roles and act

out the story using props, puppets, toys, costumes, or just by pretending. For example, here is a possible sequence from *The Gingerbread Man* retold by Bonnie Dobkin:

Day 1. Read *The Gingerbread Man*. Discuss the characters. Have the children pick one of the characters and make a statue of that character.

Day 2. Read *The Gingerbread Man* and discuss the plot. Create character statues again. Teach the children how to do pretend running. Teach the rules for acting out stories.

Day 3. Before the lesson, choose who will act as the little old lady, little old man, and the gingerbread man. Read *The Gingerbread Man* and have the children join in on the first chorus. Explain that you will be acting out part of the story after you read the book. Have the "actors" join you in the front of the rug. Remind the children of what the audience does. Act out the story up to the point where the gingerbread man runs out of the house and the little old man and the little old woman run after him and try to catch him. Have the children chant the chorus with you.

Day 4. Before the lesson, choose who will act all the parts. There are eight characters. Gather the children and review the rules for story play. Call up the characters to the front of the rug and remind children of the audience's role. Act out the entire story, prompting the children as needed. Have the children chant the chorus after each character tries to catch the gingerbread man. At the end of the session, review what the children did well and remind them of any rules they need to work on better.

Day 5. Repeat the same lesson as Day 4. Continue on other days, encouraging the children to speak in character as they act out the story

Once children are experienced with story play and know the procedures, the process can be done in a couple of days or extended over longer periods of time as part of curriculum units.

# Why Use Story Play?

Dramatic play is a rich environment for literacy learning, especially language comprehension (Rand & Morrow, 2021). Children develop language, especially vocabulary, through play as well as narrative competence, and the ability to use academic language. In addition, children who use thematic play based on stories understand and remember those stories better. They also develop a sense of story structure that helps them to understand all stories better, not just those that they have acted out. Zosh, et al., (2019) use the term, "guided play" to describe dramatic play that is supported by adults and more structured than free play. Studies show that literacy learning during play is highest when the teacher supports and guides the play, rather than letting the children play freely.

Story play was developed as a combination of two research-based strategies: read aloud experiences and guided play. The story play technique helps by improving literacy and language skills in

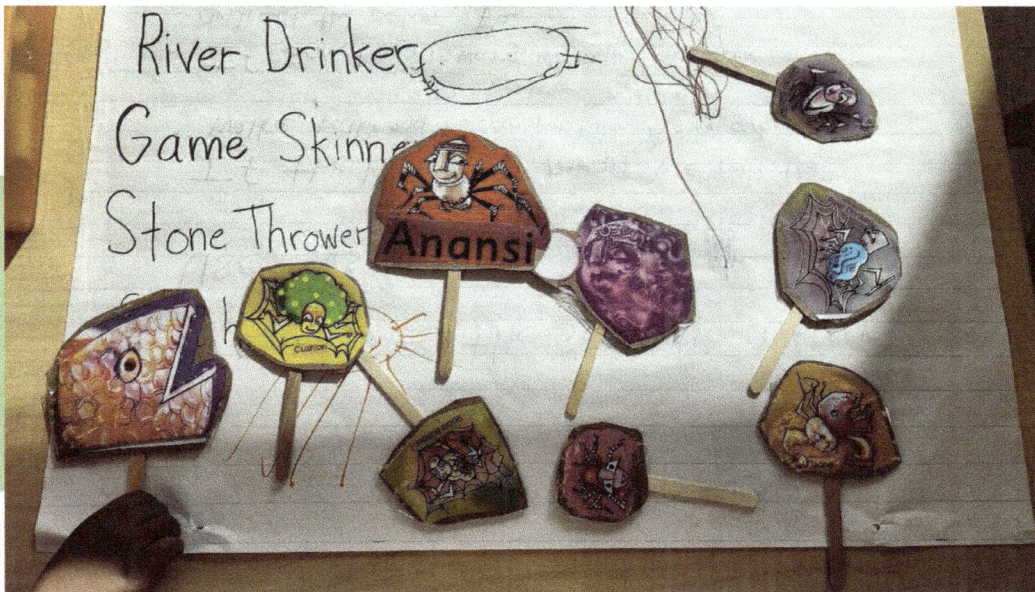

preschool through 1st grade by adding a 10-minute guided play session after reading a book to children. The table on the following page highlights recent research studies that directly support story play. As you can see, adding a 10-minute play session, guided by the teacher, increases the depth of vocabulary, expressive oral language skills, narrative comprehension, and other literacy skills. In addition to the studies listed, Cervetti, et al., (2020) provide an up-to-date review of the research literature that shows the importance of language comprehension in reading development. By helping children improve their early language development, we are preparing them to be strong readers.

# Story Play Research

| Research Study | Summary and Outcomes |
| --- | --- |
| Dickinson, et al, (2019). *Teaching for breadth and depth of vocabulary knowledge: Learning from explicit and implicit instruction and the storybook* | Preschool children from low-income families were read two books with sixteen target words. Following the read aloud, children played with replica props related to the story theme for ten minutes. Results showed that children acquire information they need to construct word meanings from hearing words multiple times as the story is read as well as during discussions and play that reinforce their understanding of the story events. |
| Dickinson, et al, (2019). *Effects of teacher-delivered book reading and play on vocabulary learning and self-regulation among low-income preschool children* | The intervention included two groups of preschoolers: book reading with teacher-directed activities and book reading with play. In the book reading alone, the teacher used definitions, gestures, and pictures to teach vocabulary. In the play session, the teacher led play with story-related figurines while using target vocabulary. Both conditions resulted in large gains on receptive and expressive knowledge of the target vocabulary words. |
| Hadley and Dickinson (2019). *Cues for word learning during shared book-reading and guided play in preschool* | The teacher read two informational texts to small groups of preschoolers and then added a 10-minute play session. After two months, the number of responsive interactions between adults and children during play showed a positive and significant association with growth in vocabulary. |
| Toub, et al. (2018). *The language of play: Developing preschool vocabulary through play following shared book reading* | This study tested three interventions with preschool children: book reading combined with 1) free play, 2) guided play, 3) directed play in eight sessions over two weeks in small groups. Children in both guided and directed play showed more gains in receptive and expressive knowledge of target words. |
| Nicolopoulou, et al., (2015). *Using a narrative- and play-based activity to promote low-income preschoolers' oral language, emergent literacy, and social competence* | A storytelling and story acting practice was integrated into the curriculum for six preschool classes. The children were compared to others from classrooms that used their typical curriculum. The children who experienced storytelling and story acting improved in narrative comprehension, print and word awareness, pretend abilities, self-regulation, and reduced play disruption. |

# Planning for Story Play

The following steps will help you get started planning for story play. It's helpful to begin with small steps and add more to your story play as you and your children get comfortable.

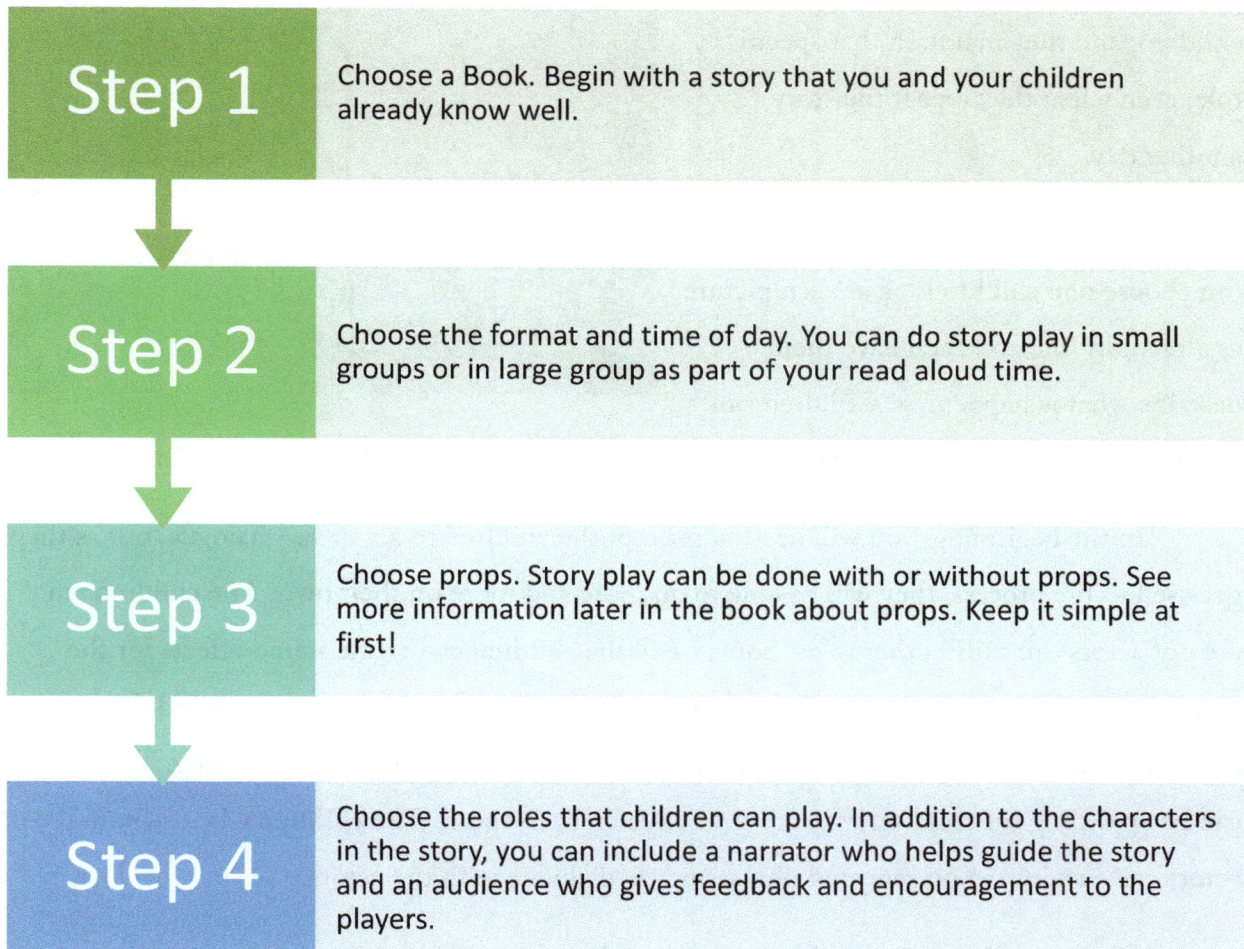

| Step 1 | Choose a Book. Begin with a story that you and your children already know well. |
|---|---|
| Step 2 | Choose the format and time of day. You can do story play in small groups or in large group as part of your read aloud time. |
| Step 3 | Choose props. Story play can be done with or without props. See more information later in the book about props. Keep it simple at first! |
| Step 4 | Choose the roles that children can play. In addition to the characters in the story, you can include a narrator who helps guide the story and an audience who gives feedback and encouragement to the players. |

Now you are ready to carry out the Story Play activity!

Begin story play by reading the book aloud as you normally would. Focus especially on any vocabulary words you want to explain. Some teachers make a chart of the target words to learn. Review who the characters are, and as appropriate, other aspects of the plot, such as the problem and solution.

Once the children are familiar with the story, assign the roles to the children. Some teachers do this randomly, or they change the roles each time they act out the story. Other teachers assign the roles to children, and they maintain that specific role, even when they repeat the story another day.

If you want to use a narrator, you can choose one child to look at each picture as a memory cue and then have them describe what is happening. Children can often memorize simple, repetitive stories or use their own words to describe the actions.

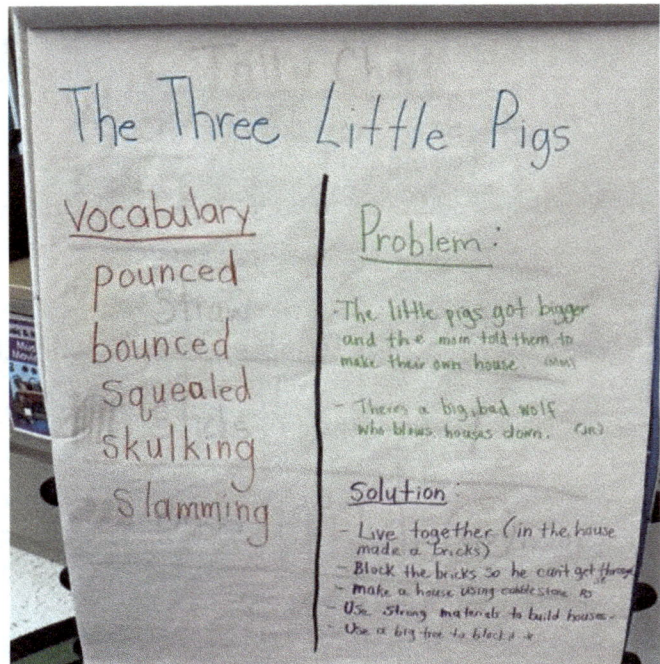

**The Three Little Pigs**

| Vocabulary | Problem: |
|---|---|
| pounced | - The little pigs got bigger and the mom told them to make their own house. (SW) |
| bounced | - There's a big bad wolf who blows houses down. (SW) |
| squealed | |
| skulking | Solution: |
| slamming | - Live together (in the house made a bricks) |
| | - Block the bricks so he can't get through |
| | - Make a house using cobblestone ro |
| | - Use strong materials to build houses |
| | - Use a big tree to block it |

In the beginning, you will need to prompt the children to act or say dialogue, but as they get used to the process, they will be able to do more and more on their own. The children who are not actors can fulfill other roles. Some or all the children can create sound effects for the story by using rhythm sticks or bells, or making the sounds of rushing water, or wind. I have seen children also take the role of trees, sand, rocks, and other aspects of the setting. These roles can be appealing for children who are shy or reluctant to speak. The children who are non-actors can also join in on repeated phrases or say dialogue with the actors.

*Frequency.* Because you will want to read the story multiple times, each story play can last a week or more. Most teachers who are using story play plan a new story each month.

*Children with Special Needs.* Story play can be beneficial for children who are non-verbal or who are learning English. Think about what actions children could perform who are non-verbal. Can they move like jellyfish? Can they stand up and hold Pete the Cat's button? Can they pretend to run after the gingerbread man? Planning for non-verbal actions can make the story play more accessible. In a similar way, you may have children who cannot move like the characters, but they could chime in on dialogue, or they could hold up a picture of a tree as the setting. Children who cannot sustain the attention needed to participate could join the group for a few minutes of story play. Sometimes children are reluctant to get involved and prefer to watch. They might be supported with a partner. Buddies can work together as one role, shadowing each other and saying the lines or doing the actions together.

*Prompting Students.* To get the children started with the story play, or to help children use dialogue or move the action along, try the following prompts:

---

*What happens first in our story?*

*What happens now?*

*What is the problem in our story?*

*Can you show how the character is feeling?*

*How would that character move? (walk, talk)*

*Let's hear the sound of the* _____

*What's the word for that (prompt use of vocabulary)*

---

**Small Group Story Play.** Instead of acting out the story during the read aloud, some teachers used small group time to reenact the story that they read to the whole group. For example, in the photo below, the children are reenacting The Three Little Pigs.

# Managing Behaviors During Story Play

Like any activity in the classroom, it's important to plan ahead to prevent behavior problems from arising during story play. Here are some ideas for avoiding challenges:

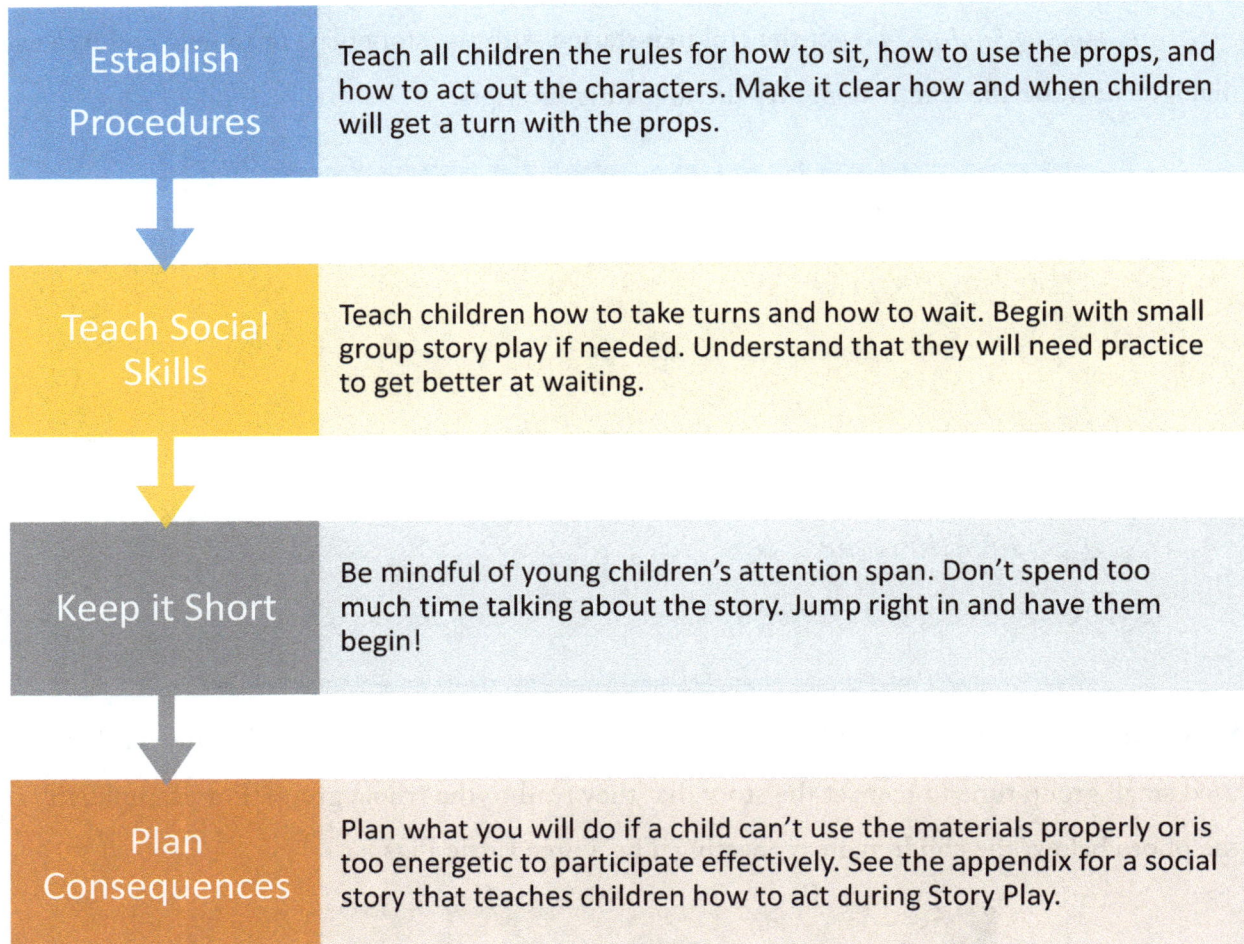

| | |
|---|---|
| **Establish Procedures** | Teach all children the rules for how to sit, how to use the props, and how to act out the characters. Make it clear how and when children will get a turn with the props. |
| **Teach Social Skills** | Teach children how to take turns and how to wait. Begin with small group story play if needed. Understand that they will need practice to get better at waiting. |
| **Keep it Short** | Be mindful of young children's attention span. Don't spend too much time talking about the story. Jump right in and have them begin! |
| **Plan Consequences** | Plan what you will do if a child can't use the materials properly or is too energetic to participate effectively. See the appendix for a social story that teaches children how to act during Story Play. |

Children with poor self-regulation can benefit from visuals of how to behave, or extra practice with the props or acting out roles in a one-on-one setting. Some children are better regulated when they sit on a chair to be part of the audience. Other children with high energy can participate by holding a picture that's part of the setting or making sound effects.

If children misbehave, first use reminders of the rules. If needed, take away the prop gently or remove the child from the story area, and let them know with a neutral voice that they will have a turn to try again another day. Use the social story in the appendix, "*How we Do Story Play in Our Classroom*" to help them learn how to behave and practice.

# Props: Choosing and Making Materials

There are a variety of ways that you can find, make, or choose props. First, remember that props are not always needed. For example, we often act out *One Dog Canoe* by Mary Casanova without any props. The story takes place on a lake and there is a canoe paddled by a girl and a variety of animals who jump in the canoe. When acting out this story, we make the read aloud rug the canoe, then we assign the roles to various students who respond to the dialogue and pretending to jump in the canoe when appropriate. It's engaging and effective with no props. That said, props are helpful visual reminders of the characters and actions in the story, and the children enjoy them.

**Classroom Items.** Some stories lend themselves to items that can be found around the classroom. For example, when acting out the story, *Abiyoyo* by Pete Seeger, the preschool classrooms used a plastic ukulele from their music center, a chair, plastic cup, a plastic saw, ironing board from the housekeeping area, and a plastic magic wand.

**Finger Puppets.** An easy way to designate characters is with puppets. These can be simple paper cut outs, such as the finger puppets on the left that children colored themselves.

**Stick Puppets.** Another simple type of puppet is a stick puppet. Any cut out of the characters can be glued or taped to sticks to create puppets. Some teachers copy pictures from the book, laminate them, and then attach the stick, as seen in this photo on the right of *The Grouchy Ladybug* by Eric Carle.

**Paper Bag Puppets.** Children can make their own puppets by drawing faces or gluing paper to paper bags. You can also copy characters from the book and attach them to paper bags for quick and easy props. This photo shows a paper bag puppet of an ox used for Hush! A Thai Lullaby by Minfong Ho.

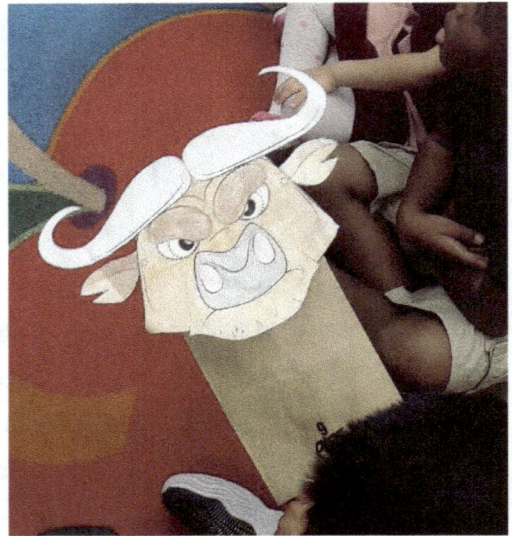

**Paper Plat Puppets and Masks.** Paper plates also work well as puppet faces, either with holes for eyes to use as a mask or without eyes to use as a puppet. Often the dollar store has paper plates already printed with animal faces.

**Costumes.** Some stories work well for simple costumes. For example, one teacher who used *The Adventures of Gary and Harry: A Tale of Two Turtles* by Lisa Matsumoto created "jellyfish" by stapling strings of ribbons on shower caps. The really did look and move like jellyfish!

**Toy Figurines.** Instead of having the children be the characters, they can manipulate figurines instead. The toys do the actions in the story, while the children talk for the characters. For example, a teacher using *The Adventures of Gary and Harry: A Tale of Two Turtles* used small sea creatures and two sets of children's mittens to have children act out the story. When enacting *The Three Billy Goats Gruff*, the children used small plastic goats and a troll and then the characters "trip-trapped" over a little wooden bridge.

**Child-made Props.**

Some props can be made by the children, extending the story play activities into art and engineering. In one classroom, the children were working on *Goldilocks and the Three Bears* for story play, and they got the idea to create the beds and chairs out of Bristol Blocks and Duplo blocks. The teacher in the photo below had the children make large round buttons to help act out *Pete the Cat and His Four Groovy Buttons* by Eric Litwin.

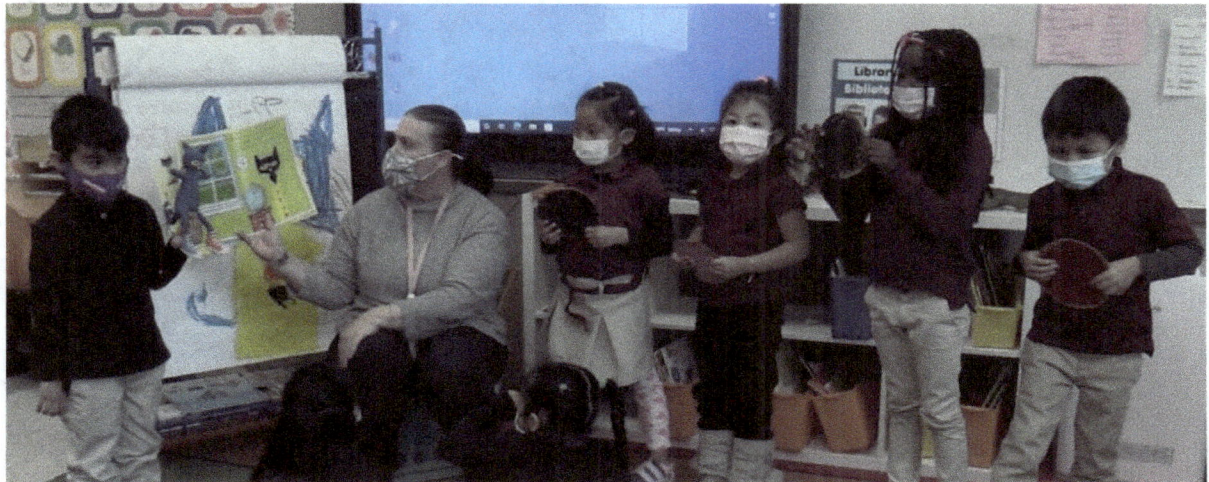

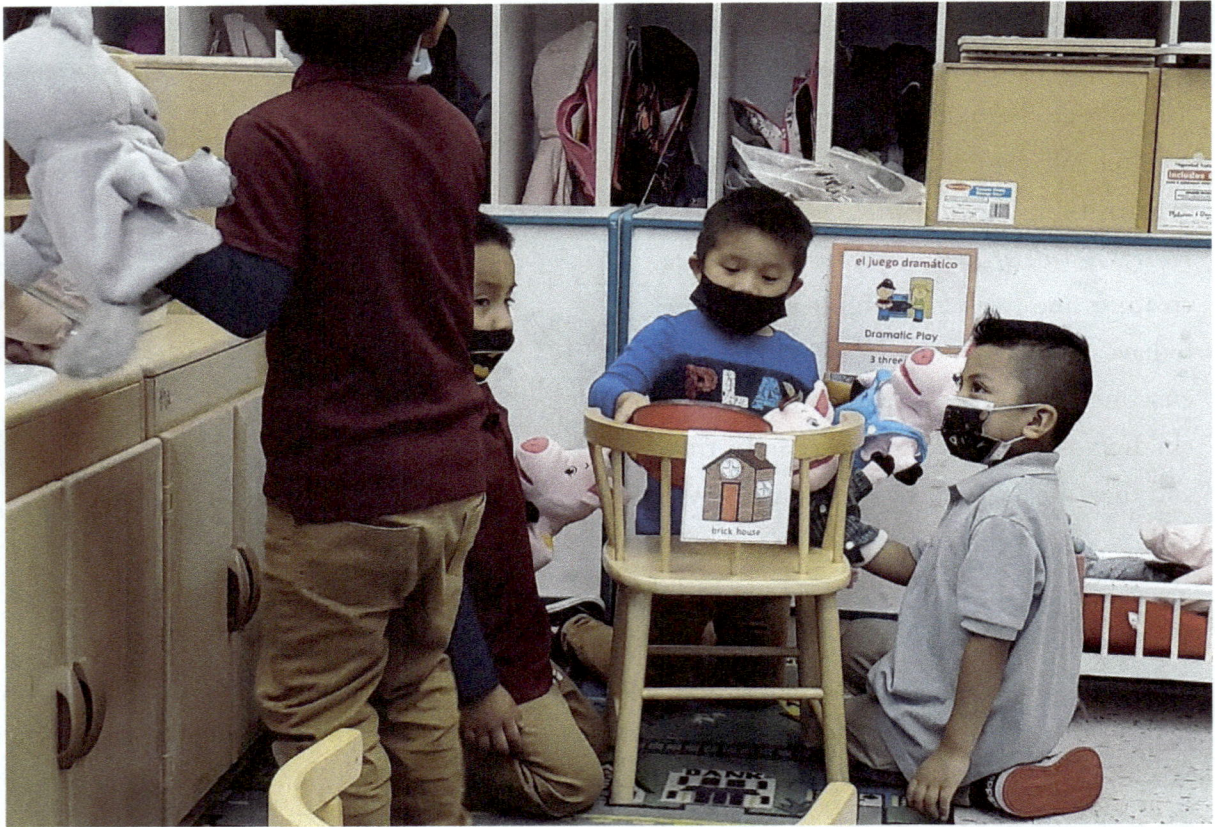

**Purchased Props:** Puppets are available from school supply stores. These puppets are typically very well made and will last a long time. They are more of a financial investment but can be a great addition to story play. In the photo above you can see children reenacting *The Three Little Pigs* with store-bought puppets during center time.

School supply stores also offer a wide variety of props to use with stories. These props are often small and intended to be used by individuals or small groups. They are also expensive, but if you can find the funds to purchase these props, they are well made and replicate the characters and items in the stories very well. The picture here shows a class using ready-made props for acting out *The Very Hungry Caterpillar* by Eric Carle.

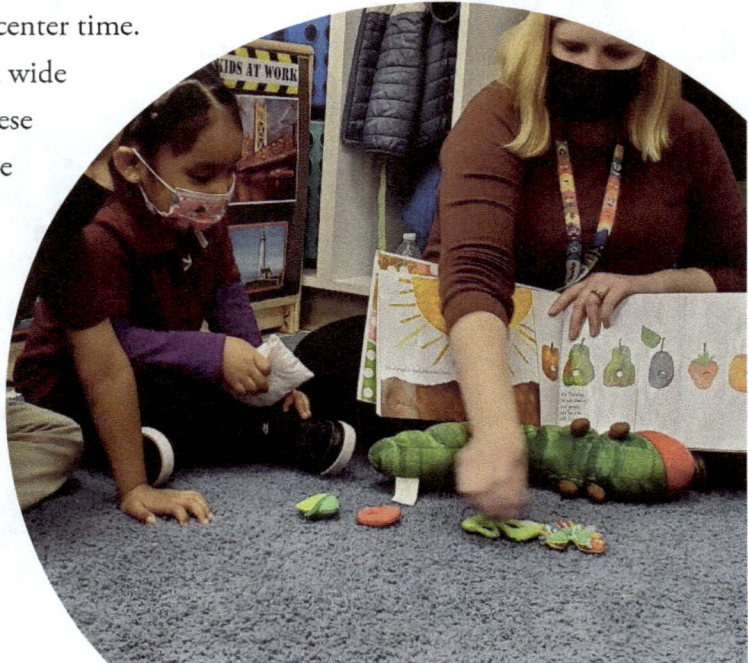

# Original Stories and Story Play

Once children are used to story play, you can introduce the idea of the children being authors themselves. The children can dictate or write their own story, either on their own or in small groups with teacher support (for more information about this type of story play, see Vivian Paley's books in the references). Then the children can act out their original stories the same way they do with published books.

For example, in one preschool classroom, four of the children got together and created their own story during center time with the teacher helping them write down their ideas. The children illustrated the story and got ready to share it with the rest of the class.

Later, during the read aloud time, the teacher and the children read their story aloud to the group. They asked for volunteers to play parts in the story. Because the story didn't have a traditional structure, the teacher invited the children to play the roles of the rainbow, the trees, the sand, and the worms. The children were excited to play these roles and acted them out with enthusiasm!

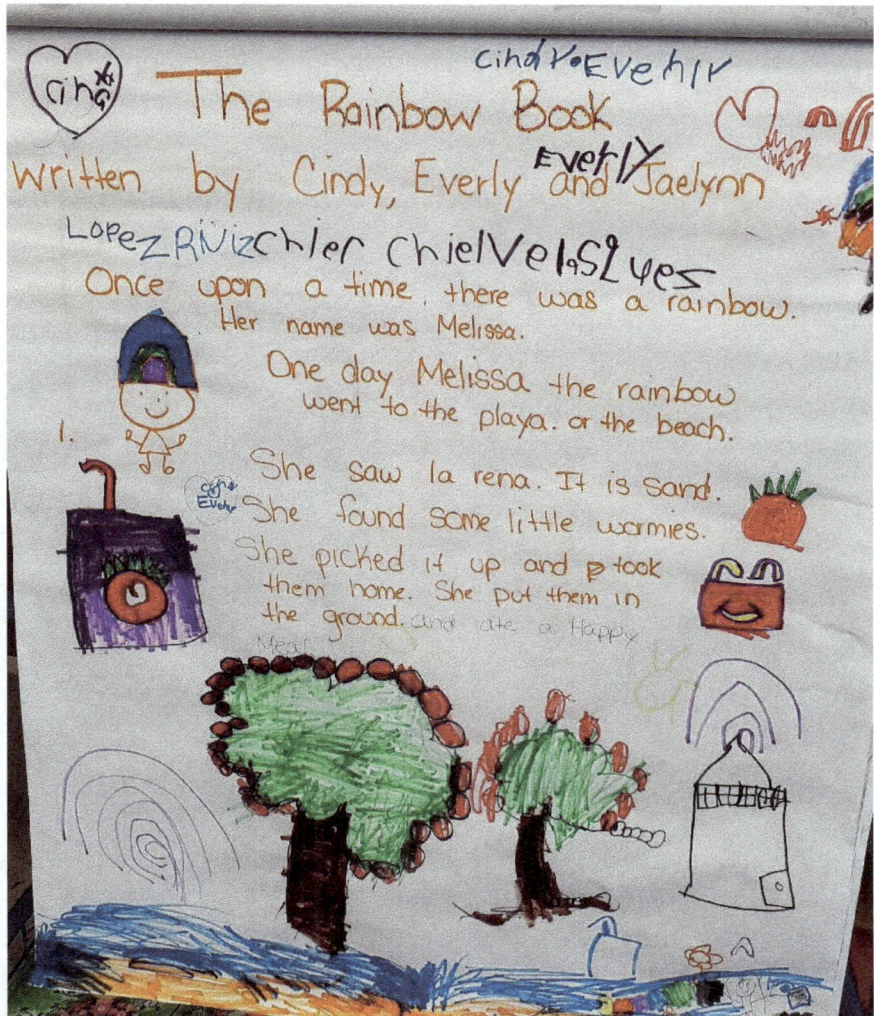

# Planning for Original Story Play

| 1. Children dictate, draw, or write their original story |
| --- |

| 2. During read aloud time, children read their story |
| --- |

| 3. Children choose who will be in their story play |
| --- |

| 4. The class acts out the original story |
| --- |

# Extending Story Play

Because story play is so rich in literacy learning, it can be extended into other parts of the curriculum. We have found that some of the extensions happen naturally without planning. For example, I was visiting one kindergarten classroom where they had used *The Gingerbread Man* for story play over the last few days. In the block area, I heard the children talking about the gingerbread man, so I went over to see what they were doing. The children had created a house for the gingerbread man to hide in so he wouldn't get eaten. In other classrooms, the children ran around the playground chanting, "you can't catch me I'm the gingerbread man!" There are also many opportunities to *plan* for story play extensions. The next section will provide ideas for integrating story play into other areas of the curriculum.

## Literacy Extensions

The book used for story play can provide the basis for studying other literacy strategies and skills. The following list shows ways that we can foster literacy through story play:

Key Ideas and Details

Retelling Stories

Story Elements: Setting, Characters, Plot, Sequencing, Problem-Solution

Comparisons to Other Books

Vocabulary

Connections to Illustrations

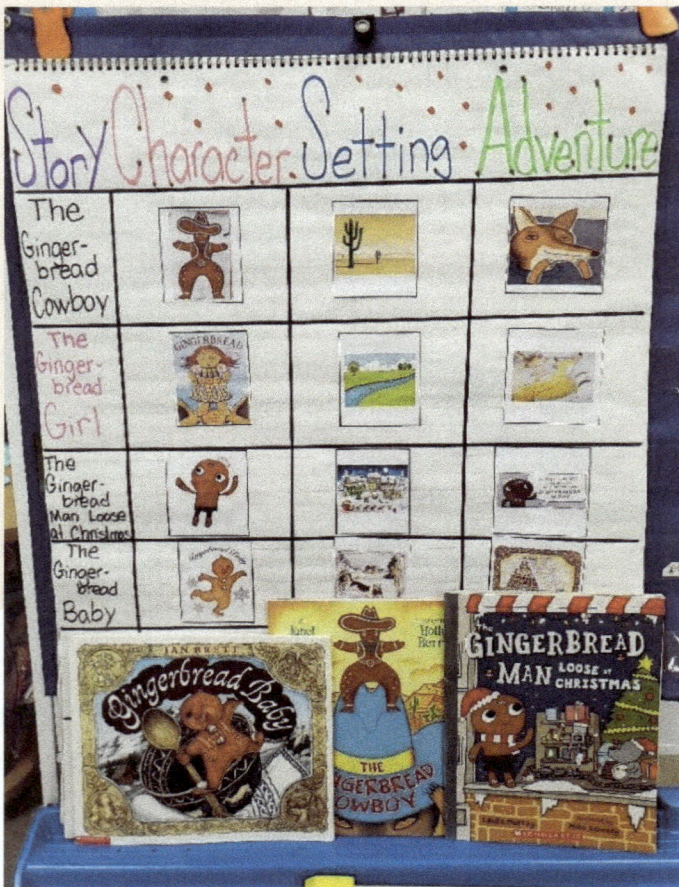

The Gingerbread Man

Literacy Extensions

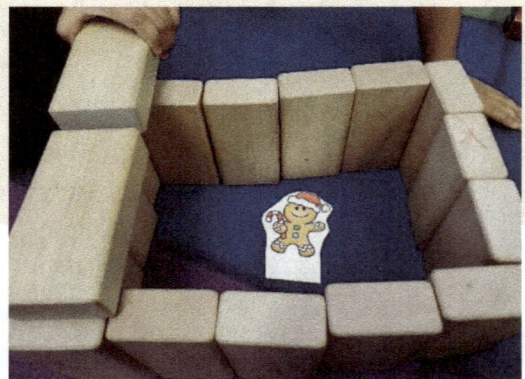

# Story Play Thematic Units

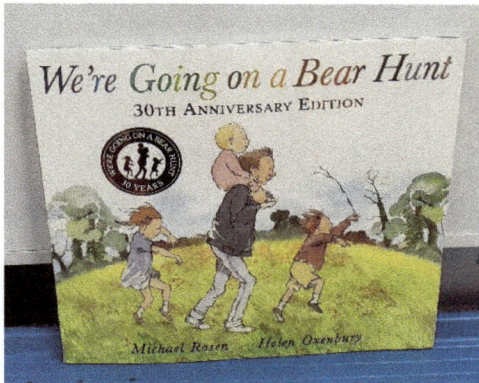

Let's look at one example of how a team of kindergarten classrooms used story play as a thematic unit. They began with the book, *We're Going on a Bear Hunt,* by Michael Rosen. First, they read the book aloud, then the teacher reviewed the various settings that take place in the story before they began to act out the story sequence. Understanding the setting is a critical for understanding the actions in the book, so this background knowledge helps the children bring the story to life with meaning.

Next, they began their story play. The teacher read the story aloud while the children performed the actions to the story all together. This is a good way of integrating story play without the need for props. It is also a low-risk way to get children who might be shy or resistant to act out the story with the support of the other students.

Because movement is a central focus of the book, having the children create the actions is supportive of their story comprehension.

As part of the unit, the children cut and pasted pictures of the plot episodes and put them in order as a way of practicing sequencing. In addition, during center time, the children had pictures of the plot episodes that they could sequence, use to retell the story, and to get ideas for journal writing.

# Library Center Props

Props, puppets, character cut outs and other items are available in a bin for the children to reenact the story on their own. This is an essential part of the story play strategy. Once the children have had the opportunity to act out the story with your support, either in whole group or small group, the next step is to encourage students to act the story on their own in the library center or the dramatic play center.

At first, you can join children in the library center to support their understanding that they can use the props to retell the story or to play with them to create new stories. The children in the photo above had just done a whole group story session of *Pete the Cat: I Love My White Shoes* by Eric Litwin. When the children picked their choices of activities for center time, the teacher reminded them that the props for Pete the Cat would be available in the library center. The first two children who choose their centers headed directly for the props! The teacher also joined them to model how to use the props and to support their independence.

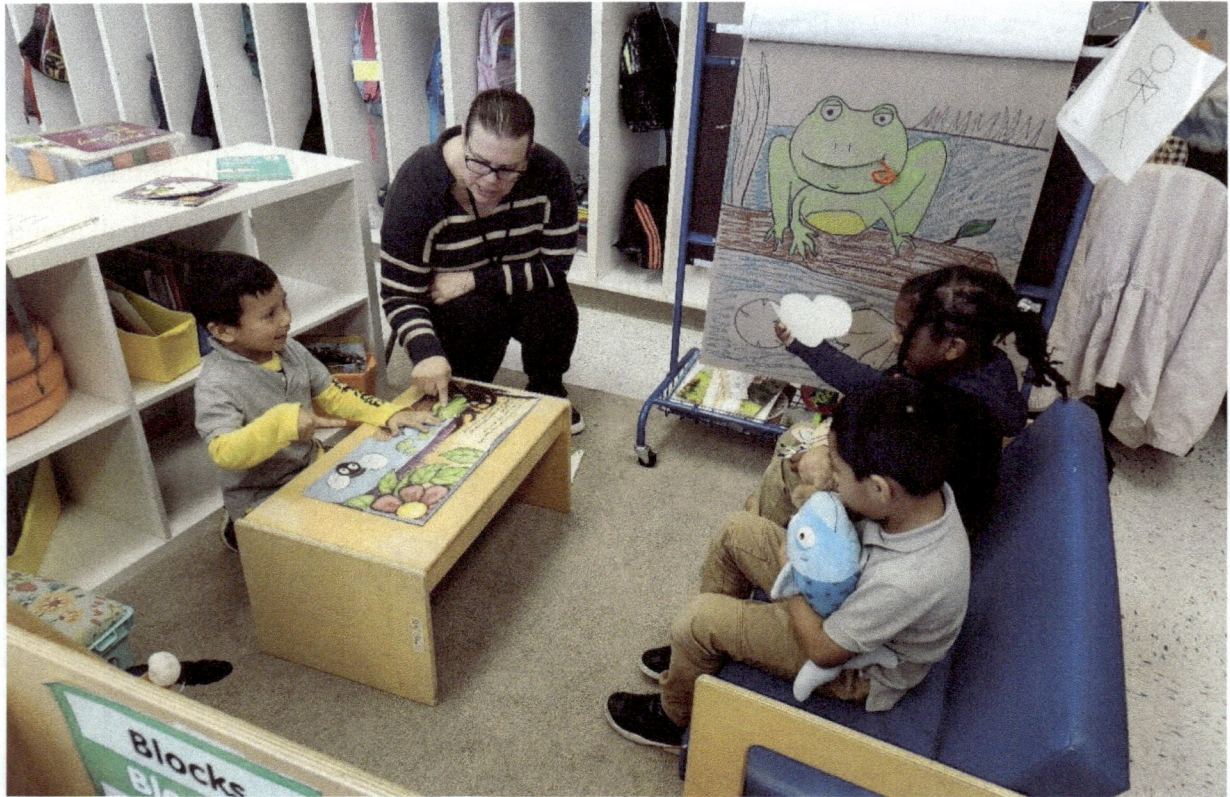

Similarly, in the photo above the children had participated in a story play session with *The Icky Sticky Frog* by Salina Yoon. The props included a large poster of the frog. The frog's mouth had a slit where they could put the animals that the frog ate. The teacher rolled the poster to the library area and sat for a few minutes to support the children's independent play with the props. Once the children are familiar with the props and the story, they enjoy working with the props on their own, acting out the story, using the different character voices, and pretending with new plot episodes.

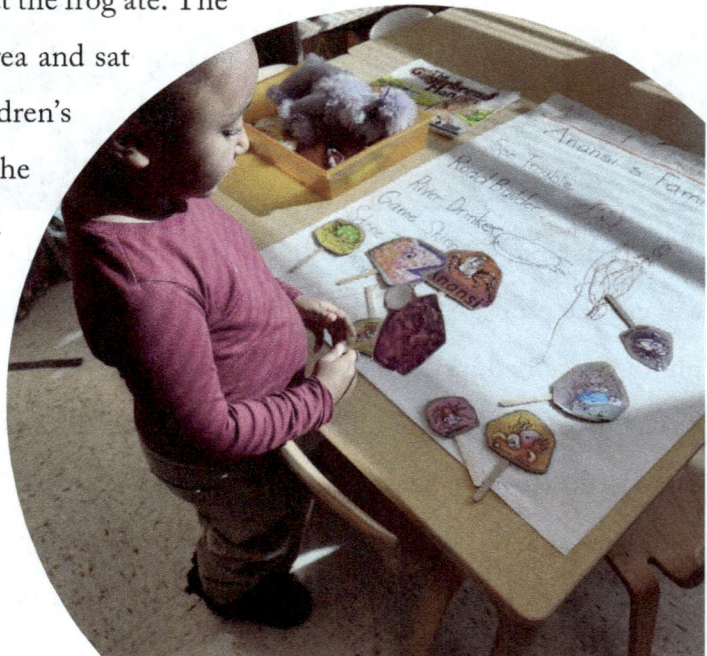

# Dramatic Play Center

The dramatic play center is the closest connection to story play because children can reenact the story on their own without the support of the teacher. Props from the book are available for students to create dramatic play based on the story book. For example, after reading and reenacting *The Gingerbread Man*, the dramatic play center included a bakery for kindergarten students to bake gingerbread cookies and pretend to be the Old Woman and Old Man.

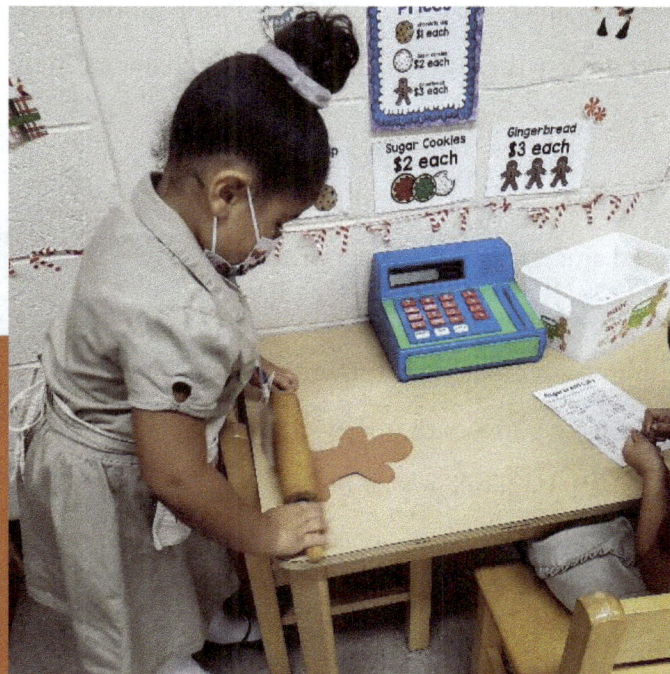

# Art and Story Play

Children can create props and other items for the story play. As seen above, one child drew a large poster of Pete the Cat to use as the main character in their story play.

In another classroom, the children colored small finger puppets for their gingerbread man story play. The children each created their own set of finger puppets that they could use independently or during small group play.

Students can also create scenery and props relating to the settings of the story play sessions. For example, the children in one classroom created the houses for the *Three Little Pigs* and another classroom created the bridge for *The Three Billy Goats Gruff*.

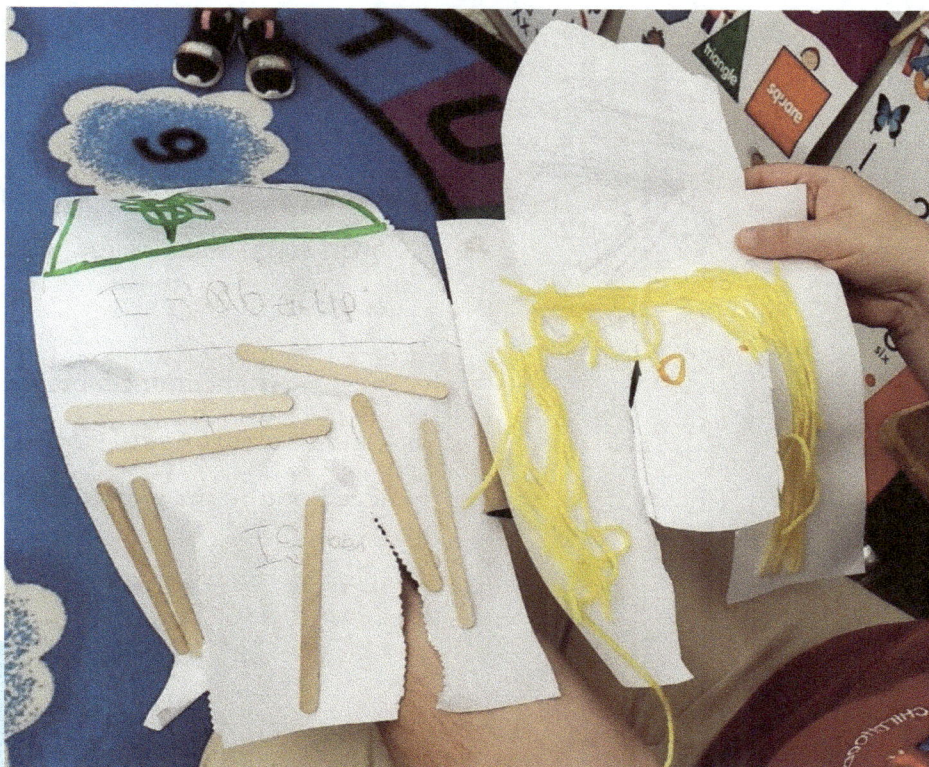

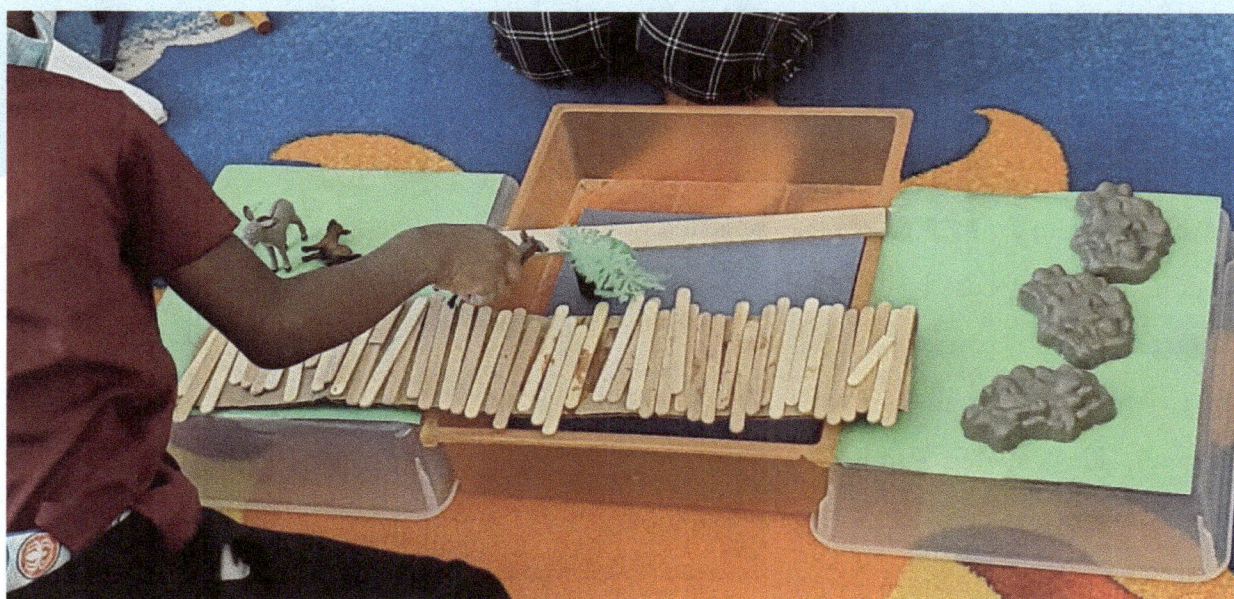

# Writing and Story Play

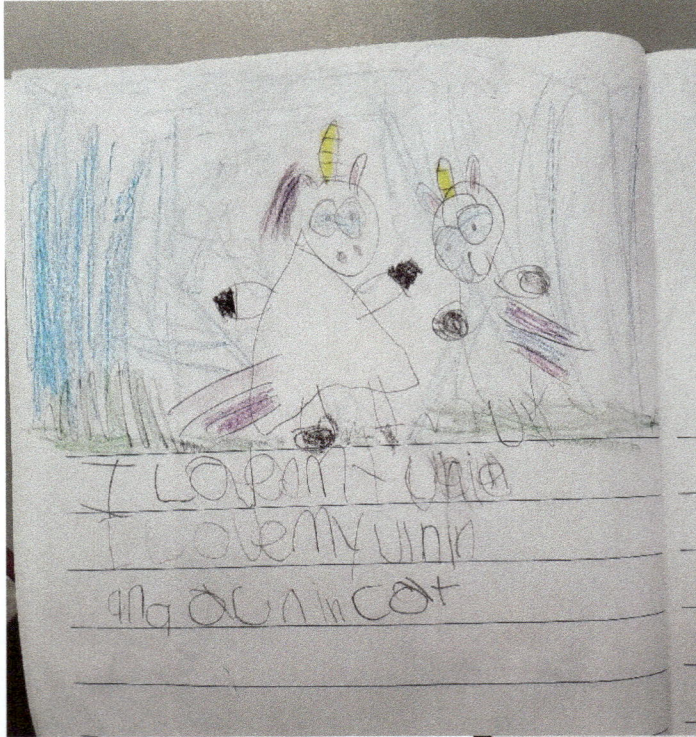

Writing can be connected to story play in a variety of ways. Children can write in their journals about the stories they are acting out by retelling those stories, adding on to them, or developing their own story that might relate to the original.

As mentioned before, students can also write original stories that can be acted out by small groups or the whole class. In the photo here, a group of children created a collaborative story about a squirrel in a tree that they dictated to the teacher.

One kindergarten class integrated writing by creating a Playbill program for their story play session. They focused on the characters in the story and each child wrote their name in the program. They invited families to come see their play.

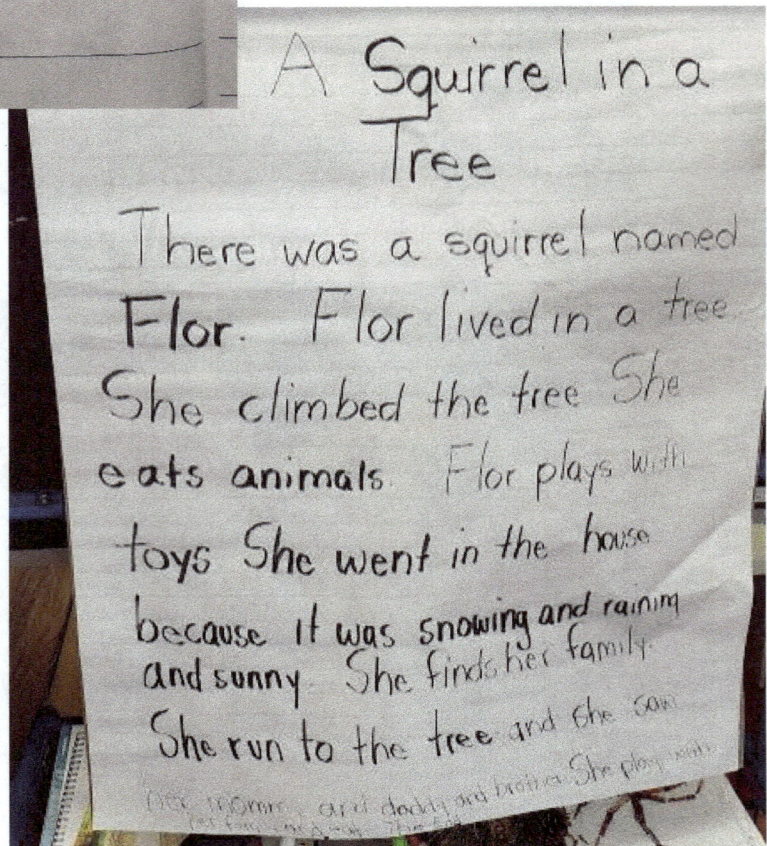

Welcome to our Story /
Bienvenidos a nuestro cuento
The Snow Tree
by Caroline Repchuk

Story play program for *The Snow Tree* created by a kindergarten class

Personajes (en la secuencia de aparencia)
Characters (in order of appearance)

Little Bear/ Osito — Ed Uah
Lince/Lynx — Axel
Ardillas/ Squirrels — Jose Hernan be Manuel
Azulejo/ Blue Jay — Uriel
Visón/mink — Michael
Mapache/raccon — Broyder, Esxhon
Reno/reindeer — Josias
Pajarito/Bunting — Heather/ Britney
Zorro arctico/Arctic fox — Derek
Alce/Moose — Ashley

Children can also use story play to learn more about writing stories. By using the story elements they have learned during story play, they can create original stories and work on the mechanics of writing as well. In these examples, kindergarten children studied fairy tales through story play, and then created their own.

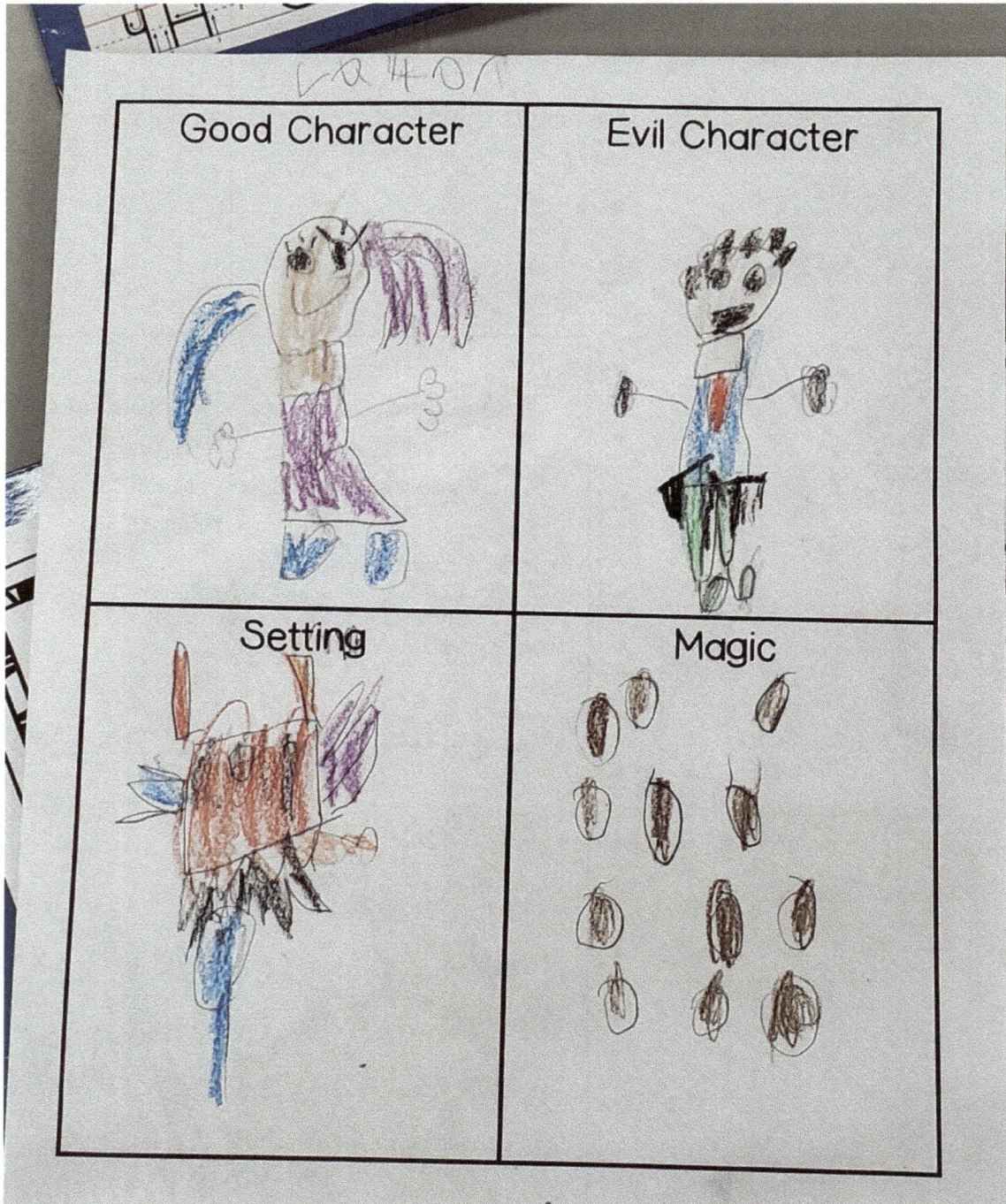

Story Play: Bringing Books to Life in the Classroom

# Science and Engineering and Story Play

Many children's books lend themselves to problem solving and using the design process to come up with new solutions. For example, in one classroom, the children acted out the story of the Three Little Pigs and focused on the problem of the wolf. In the design process, the first step is to empathize with the people (or animals in this case) to truly understand the problem. The next step is to define the problem, which was the strengths of the wolf's huffing and puffing. After that, the children built protypes of houses that would be strong enough to stand up to the wolf, and then the class tested them out with a fan to simulate the wolf's huffing and puffing. This is what it looked like:

**Design Process Steps with The Three Little Pigs:**

1. **Empathize:** Children acted out the story to understand the pig's problem.

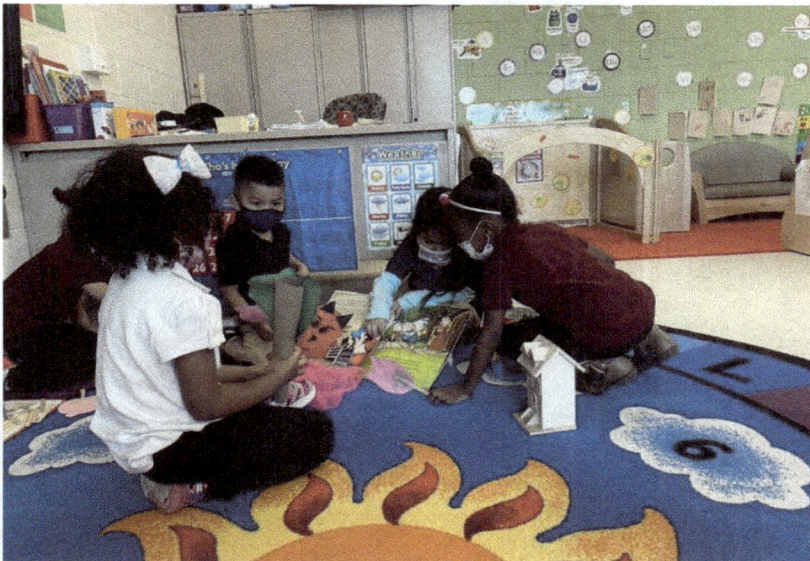

2. **Identify the problem.** The big, bad wolf blows houses down.

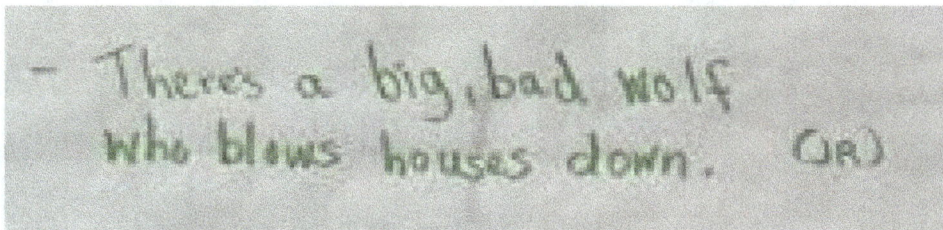

- There's a big, bad wolf who blows houses down. (JR)

3.  **Think up possible solutions.** Chidlren brainstormed what materials they could use to make houses.

4.  **Create prototypes.** Children created houses from different materials.

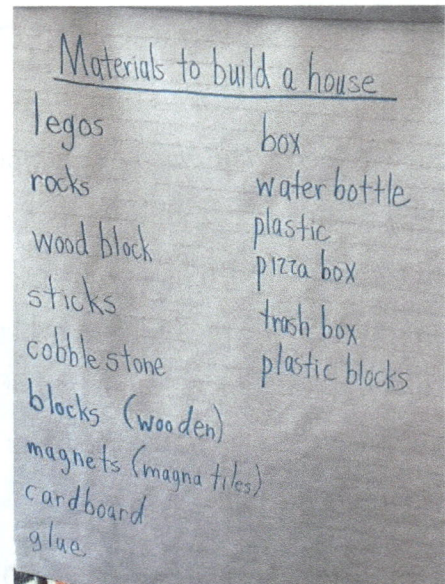

Materials to build a house
legos                    box
rocks                    water bottle
wood block               plastic
sticks                   pizza box
cobble stone             trash box
blocks (wooden)          plastic blocks
magnets (magna tiles)
cardboard
glue

5.  **Test Solutions.** Children used a fan to simulate the big, bad wolf and tested the strength of their houses.

The children also focused on science and engineering when they acted out The Three Billy Goats Gruff. They identified the problems and wrote them down and then brainstormed ideas for alternative solutions.

Some of their solutions included making a trap from the Troll, blocking the trap with tape, step on floaties to get across, build a big boat, make a giant robot to walk across the river, and make another bridge.

Finally the children set out to create prototypes to test their solutions.

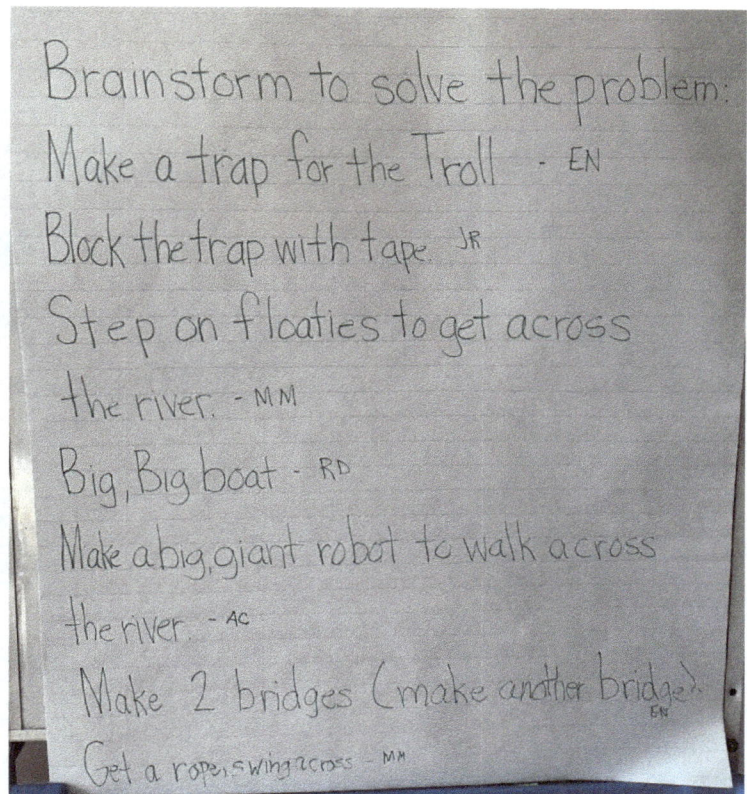

Brainstorm to solve the problem:
Make a trap for the Troll - EN
Block the trap with tape. JR
Step on floaties to get across the river. - MM
Big, Big boat - RD
Make a big, giant robot to walk across the river. - AC
Make 2 bridges (make another bridge). EN
Get a rope, swing across - MM

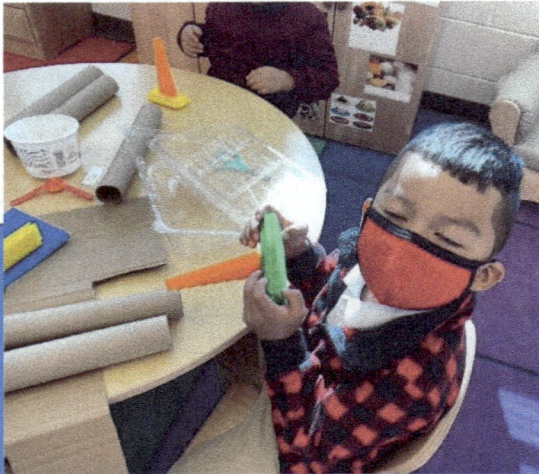

Story Play: Bringing Books to Life in the Classroom

# The Teacher as a Play Partner

The research on the value of play in the classroom has shown the *guided play* primes academic learning better than free play (Zosh, et al., 2018). Researchers consider play as a spectrum in which free play is at one end and direct instruction on the other end. Too often, play has been removed from early childhood, especially in kindergarten and first grade because administrators, policy makers, and sometimes teachers think of play as "free play" in which children have full control of choosing and carrying out activities. Play is often contrasted with academic work as if they were opposites. In reality, as this graphic shows, play has a range of possibilities and academic learning can happen in the context of play. While free play has it place and value, there are times when guided play can be a more appropriate choice for classroom learning, especially in the primary grades.

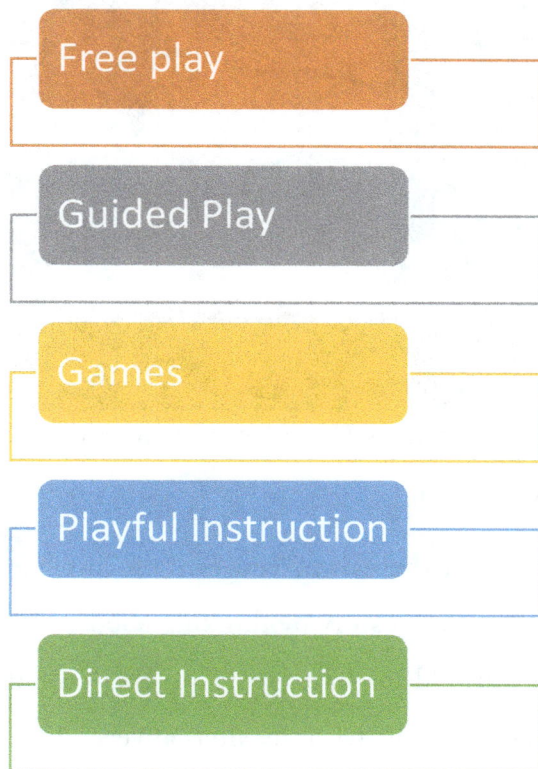

Free play

Guided Play

Games

Playful Instruction

Direct Instruction

Story play provides a perfect opportunity for guided play in which the teacher is a play partner. When we first introduce story play, we are on the continuum closer to direct instruction. This is important for teaching vocabulary and making sure that children have the background knowledge to comprehend the story. As the children gain more experience with story play, we move on the continuum to playful instruction, in which we direct the children's actions but there is a playful element in acting out the story. Our ultimate goal is to have the children take more initiative and direct the play themselves, with us there to provide support. This happens best during center time in which the children are able to use the props and book to reenact the story.

*Providing Guidance.* One way to provide guidance when children are acting out the stories on their own is to simply ensure that the props and materials are available for the children to use on their own. Then you can observe closely for when you might be needed. If the children can manage the story enactment on their own, then we don't need to intervene.

Another strategy is to help the children remember the sequence of the story by asking, "What comes next? Let's look at the book and see what happens." You can also prompt the children to say dialogue from the story, or to show some of the emotions from the book.

One of the best ways to support the play is to act out one of the roles from the story yourself. That way you can model how to act out the character and be a collaborative peer instead of a director. The children love having you as an actor in their drama!

When children are comfortable acting out stories on their own, you can also provide guidance to get them to be more creative. They can add on to the story by thinking about what would happen next, or they could come up with an alternative ending. The children could add additional characters, or even change the setting. By providing art materials close to or in the library area, the children can also make their own props with your guidance. This creativity can spill over into their writing as they create their own stories or modify stories they know.

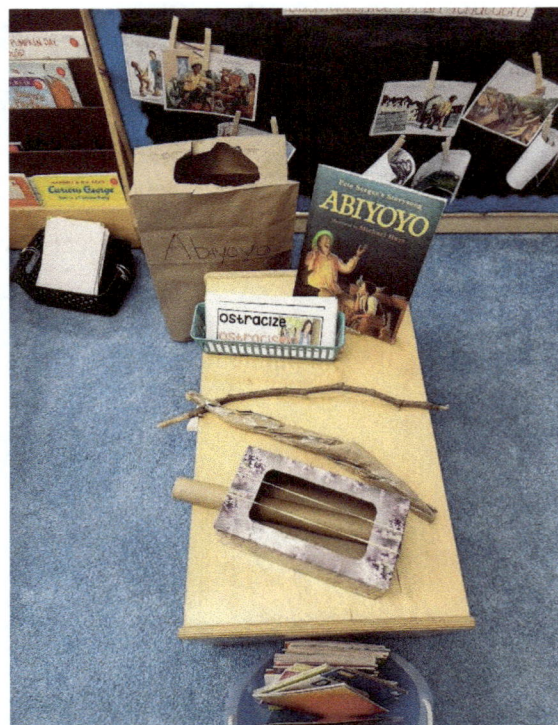

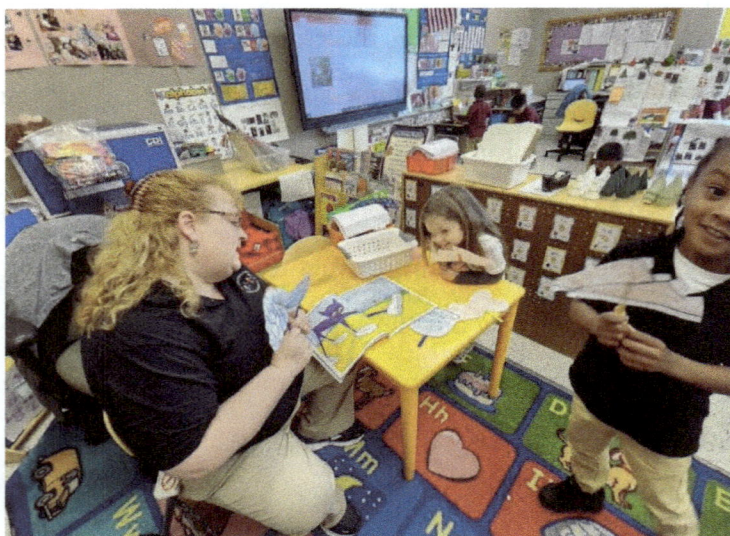

# Assessing Story Play

Story play is an excellent context to assess children's language, literacy, and social development. The story play activities can be assessed on its own and the children's progress can be tracked each quarter over the course of the school year. Alternatively, the story play activities can be included as part of other developmental assessments.

## Story Play Assessment Rubric

| | Not Yet Begun | In Progress | Mastered |
|---|---|---|---|
| Identifies Settings | | | |
| Identifies Characters | | | |
| Acts out characters appropriately | | | |
| Uses dialogue from the story | | | |
| Identifies story plot episodes | | | |
| Demonstrates an understanding of target vocabulary words (such as acting them out or pointing to pictures of them) | | | |
| Creates an original story | | | |
| Uses target vocabulary words | | | |
| Collaborates with others | | | |
| Waits for a turn | | | |
| Shares materials | | | |
| Initiates story play independently or with a small group | | | |

For example, the following preschool developmental indicators from COR Advantage and Teaching Strategies Gold align with story play:

## COR Advantage Items for Story Play Observations

### I. Approaches to Learning

    A. Initiative and planning

    B. Problem solving with materials

### II. Social and Emotional Development

    F. Building relationships with other children

    G. Community

    H. Conflict Resolution

### IV. Language, Literacy and Communication

    L. Speaking

    M. Listening and comprehension

    Q. Book enjoyment and knowledge

### VI. Creative Arts

    AA. Pretend Play

### IX. English Language Learning

    II. Listening to and understanding English

Story Play: Bringing Books to Life in the Classroom

**Teaching Strategies Gold Objectives for Development and Learning**

**Story Play Observations**

### Social-Emotional

3. Participates cooperatively and constructively in group situations
    a. Balances needs and rights of self and others
    b. Solves social problems

### Cognitive

12. Remembers and connects experiences
    a. Recognizes and recalls
    b. Makes connections

### Literacy

18. Comprehends and responds to books and other texts
    a. Interacts during read-alouds and book conversations
    b. Uses emergent reading skills
    c. Retells stories

### The Arts

36. Explores drama through actions and language

### English Language Acquisition

37. Listening to and understanding English

38. Speaking English

Story play activities also align with the Common Core State Standards and provide a context for assessing those standards. The following table shows the kindergarten standards that can be assessed as part of story play sessions.

## Story Play and Common Core State Standards in Kindergarten

### Reading Literature

**Key Ideas and Details**

RL.K.1. With prompting and support, ask and answer questions about key details in a text (e.g., who, what, where, when, why, how).

RL.K.2. With prompting and support, retell familiar stories, including key details (e.g., who, what, where, when, why, how).

RL.K.3. With prompting and support, identify characters, settings, and major events in a story.

**Integration of Knowledge and Ideas**

RL.K.7. With prompting and support, describe the relationship between illustrations and the story in which they appear (e.g., what moment in a story an illustration depicts).

**Range of Reading and Level of Text Complexity**

RL.K.10. Actively engage in group reading activities with purpose and understanding.

### Writing

W.K.3. Use a combination of drawing, dictating, and writing to narrate a single event or several loosely linked events, tell about the events in the order in which they occurred, and provide a reaction to what happened.

# Speaking and Listening

**Presentation of Knowledge and Ideas**

SL.K.5. Add drawings or other visual displays to descriptions as desired to provide additional detail.

SL.K.6. Speak audibly and express thoughts, feelings, and ideas clearly.

# Language

**Vocabulary Acquisition and Use**

L.K.4. Determine or clarify the meaning of unknown and multiple-meaning words and phrases based on kindergarten reading and content.

    A. Identify new meanings for familiar words and apply them accurately (e.g., knowing *duck* is a bird and learning the verb to *duck*).

    B. Use the most frequently occurring affixes (e.g., -ed, -s, -ing) as a clue to the meaning of an unknown word.

L.K.5. With guidance and support from adults, explore word relationships and nuances in word meanings.

    A. Sort common objects into categories (e.g., shapes, foods) to gain a sense of the concepts the categories represent.

    B. Demonstrate understanding of frequently occurring verbs and adjectives by relating them to their opposites (antonyms).

    C. Identify real-life connections between words and their use (e.g., note places at school that are colorful).

    D. Distinguish shades of meaning among verbs describing the same general action (e.g., *walk, march, strut, prance*) by acting out the meanings.

L.K.6. Use words and phrases acquired through conversations, reading and being read to, and responding to texts.

Story Play: Bringing Books to Life in the Classroom

# Story Play Ideas

# Abiyoyo by Pete Seeger

**Characters:**

Little Boy

Boy's Father

Abiyoyo

Townspeople (as many as you like)

---

**Setting:** House and outside the town

**Suggested Props:** Dress up clothes or costume for Abiyoyo, stick for the magic wand, chair, plastic cup, ukulele

Note: A video of Pete Seeger singing and telling the story of Abiyoyo is readily available online.

---

**Target Vocabulary:**

Ukulele

Disappear

Magic Wand

Giant

Slobbery

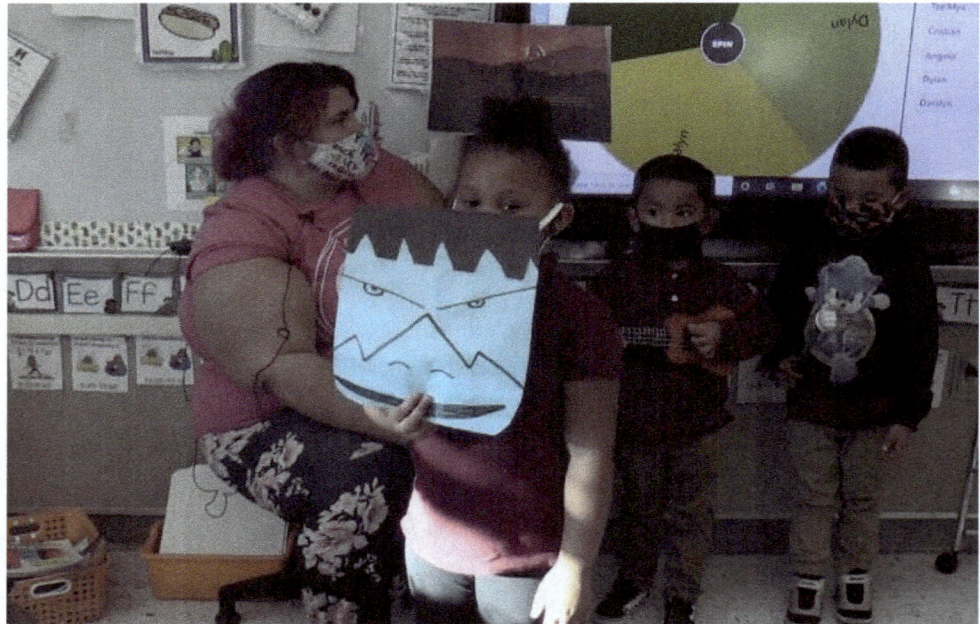

# Adventures of Gary and Harry:
# A Tale of Two Turtles by Lisa Matsumoto

**Characters:**

Gary the Turtle

Harry the Turtle

Olivia the Octopus

Herman the Hermit Crab

Lori the Lobster

Circus Performers

Clown Fish (As many as you like)

Jellyfish (As many as you like)

---

**Setting:** Ocean

**Suggested Props:** Costumes or Miniature Toys

---

**Target Vocabulary:**

Suddenly

Swallowed

Gulp

Terrified

Choked

Jellyfish

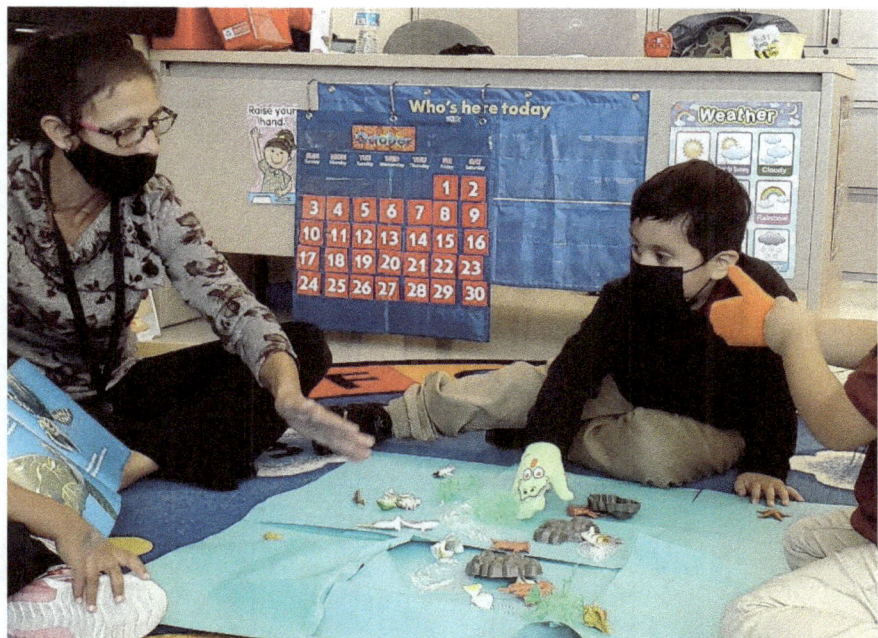

# Brown Bear, Brown Bear by Bill Martin, Jr.

**Characters:**

| | | |
|---|---|---|
| Narrator | Black Sheep | Green Frog |
| Brown Bear | Goldfish | White Dog |
| Purple Cat | Yellow Duck | Teacher |
| Blue Horse | Red Bird | |

**Setting:** Not specified; classroom at end

**Props:** Face puppets; paper bag puppets

**Target Vocabulary:** Names of animals; color words

# Chicka Chicka Boom Boom by Bill Martin, Jr. and John Archambault

**Characters:**

| Coconut Tree | Letters | Moon |
| --- | --- | --- |

**Setting:** Coconut tree, during day and night

**Props:** Tree, letters that can stick on the tree

**Target Vocabulary:**

| Told | Room | Stooped |
| --- | --- | --- |
| Meet | Tag along | Black-eyed |

# The Doorbell Rang by Pat Hutchins

**Characters:**

Ma

Victoria and Sam

Tom and Hannah

Peter and Brother

Joy and Simon

Grandma

---

**Setting:** Home

**Suggested Props:** Plates and Cookies

---

**Target Vocabulary:**

Plenty

Each

Enormous

Number words

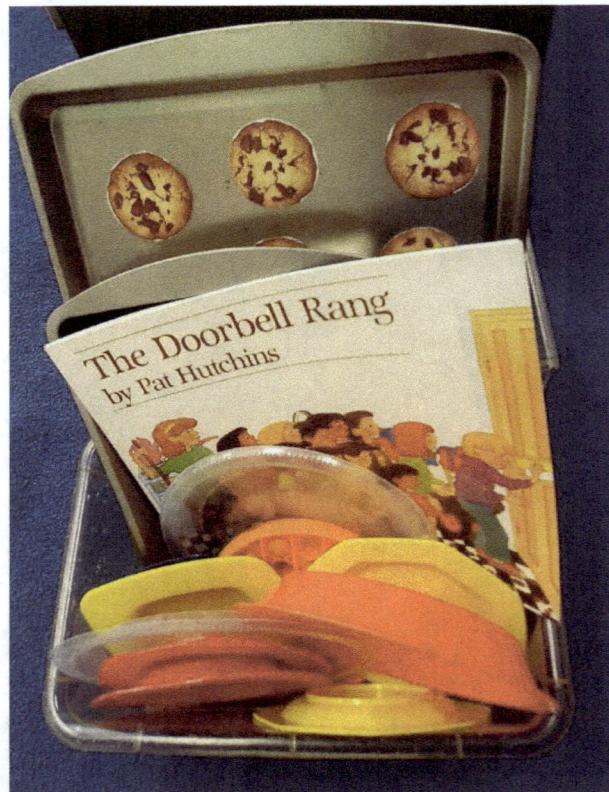

# Gingerbread Man by Bonnie Dobkin

**Characters:**

| | | |
|---|---|---|
| Little Old Woman | Officer | Horse |
| Little Old Man | Dog | Fox |
| Gingerbread Man | Cow | |

---

**Setting:** House, Town, Farm, River

**Suggested Props:** Puppets or Dress Up Clothes

---

**Target Vocabulary:**

For this story, have the children chant the refrain:

*Run, run, as fast as you can. You can't*

*catch me, I'm the Gingerbread Man!*

*I ran away from the Little Old Woman.*

*I ran away from the Little Old Man.*

*And I can run away from you, too!*

*Oh Yes, I can, I can!*

# Goldilocks and the Three Bears – Traditional

**Characters:**

Goldilocks

Mama Bear

Papa Bear

Baby Bear

**Setting:** Inside the house

**Suggested Props:** Children can make three beds and three chairs out of blocks; three bowls, or use child-size furniture

**Target Vocabulary:**

| | | |
|---|---|---|
| Locks | Forest | Porridge |
| Cottage | Dangerous | Medium |

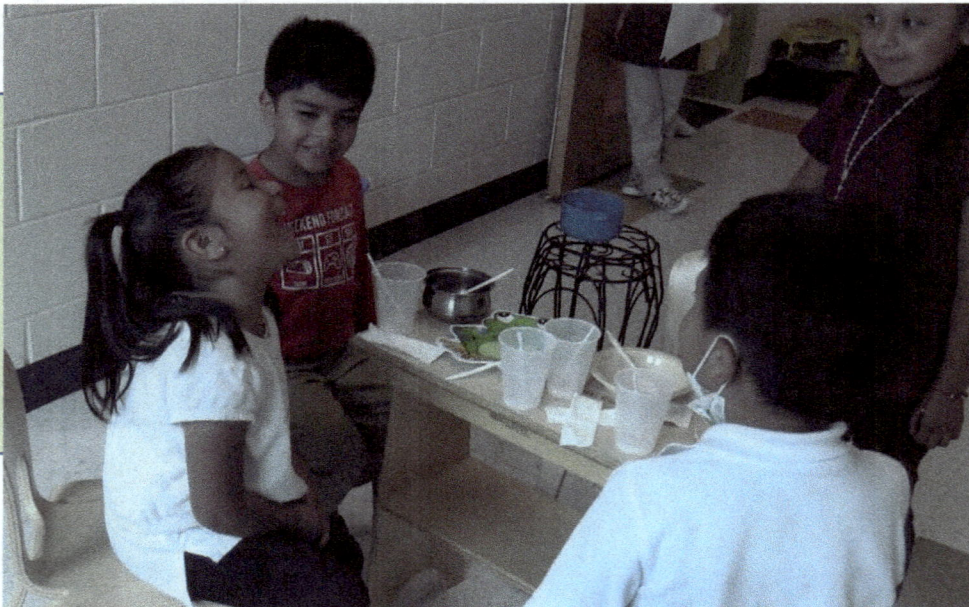

Story Play: Bringing Books to Life in the Classroom

# The Grouchy Ladybug by Eric Carle

**Characters:**

| | | |
|---|---|---|
| Grouchy Ladybug | Sparrow | Gorilla |
| Friendly Ladybug | Lobster | Rhinoceros |
| Yellow Jacket/Wasp | Skunk | Elephant |
| Stag Beetle | Boa Constrictor | Whale |
| Praying Mantis | Hyena | |

---

**Setting:** Outdoors

**Props:** Stick puppets with character cutouts

---

**Target Vocabulary:** Names of the Animals

The Grouchy Ladybug
Eric Carle

# Henny Penny - Traditional

**Characters:**

| | | |
|---|---|---|
| Henny Penny | Ducky Lucky | Cocky Locky |
| Turkey Lurkey | Goosey Loosey | Foxy Loxy |

**Setting:** Farm

**Suggested Props:** Children can draw pictures of the characters to cut out and use as stick puppets or paper plate puppets

**Target Vocabulary**

| | | |
|---|---|---|
| Acorn | Flutter | Roosting |
| Join | Pond | Distressed |

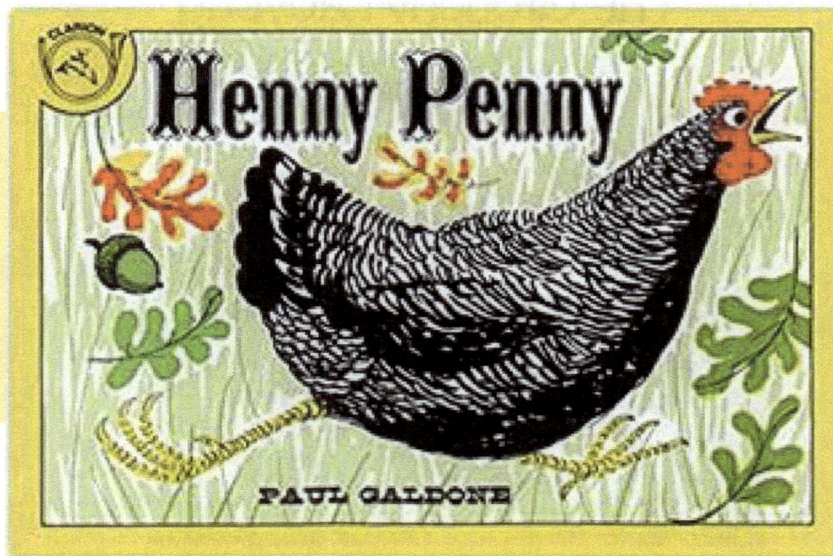

Story Play: Bringing Books to Life in the Classroom

# Hush! A Thai Lullaby by Minfong Ho

**Characters:**

| | | |
|---|---|---|
| Narrator | Cat | Duck |
| Mother | Mouse | Monkey |
| Mosquito | Frog | Water Buffalo |
| Lizard | Pig | Elephant |

**Setting:** Outside in a Thai Village

**Suggested Props:** Paper Bag or Paper Plate Puppets

**Target Vocabulary:**

| | | |
|---|---|---|
| Hush | Leaping | Sweeping |
| Creeping | Sniffling | Shrieking |
| Pepping | Beeping | Dozes |
| Squeaking | Swinging | |

# The Icky Sticky Frog by Dawn Bentley

**Characters:**

Frog                    Beetle                    Butterfly

Fly                     Grasshopper

**Setting:** Lake

**Props:** Cut outs of animals, Frog with cut out mouth

**Target Vocabulary:**

Eyed

Sticky

Slurp

Gulp

# The Little Mouse, The Red Ripe Strawberry, and the Big Hungry Bear by Don and Audrey Wood

**Characters:**

Little Mouse                    Big Hungry Bear                    Narrator

---

**Setting:** The forest

**Props:** Stuffed animals and plastic strawberry or picture cutouts

---

**Target Vocabulary:**

Tromp                           Hidden

Sniff                           Disguised

# The Mixed-Up Chameleon by Eric Carle

**Characters:**

| | | |
|---|---|---|
| Chameleon | Seal | Deer |
| Polar Bear | Flamingo | Fish |
| Elephant | Fox | People |
| Turtle | Giraffe | |

---

**Setting:** The Zoo

**Suggested Props:** Puppets or cutouts of the animals

---

**Target Vocabulary:**

| | | |
|---|---|---|
| Chameleon and other animal words | Wish | Handsome |

# One Dog Canoe by Mary Casanova

**Characters:**

| | |
|---|---|
| Girl | Wolf |
| Dog | Bear |
| Beaver | Moose |
| Loon | Frog |

**Setting:** In a canoe on a lake

**Suggested Props:** None needed. Students act out the animals.

**Target Vocabulary:**

Animal names

Pal

Scramble

Paddle

Slid

Stroked

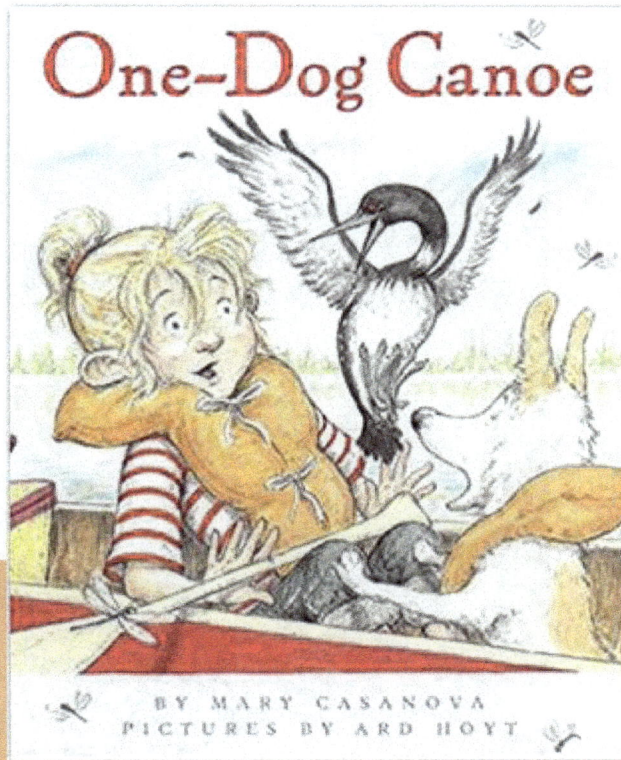

# The Paper Bag Princess by Robert Munsch

**Characters:**

Princess Elizabeth          Prince Ronald          Large Dragon

**Setting:** Castle and cave

**Suggested Props:** Paper bag clothes made by the children, crowns, hats, cutouts

**Target Vocabulary:**

Princess          Cave          Rescue

Prince          Dragon

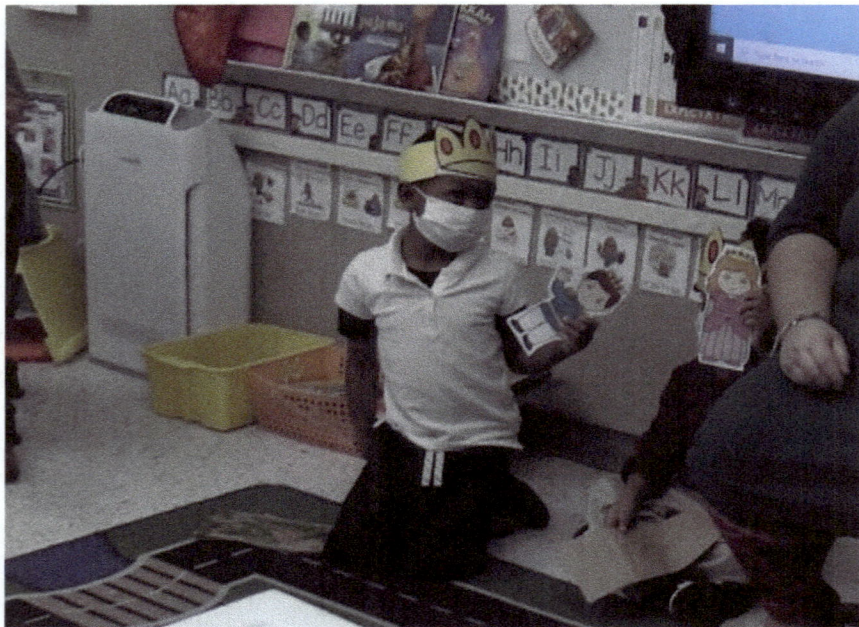

# Pete the Cat and His Four Groovy Buttons by Eric Litwin

**Characters:**

Pete the Cat                                              Four Buttons

---

**Setting:** Outside in a neighborhood

**Suggested Props:** Pete the Cat stuffed animal, cardboard buttons painted or colored by the children

---

**Target Vocabulary:**

Groovy                          Left                          Rolled

Popped                          Goodness, no!

# Pete the Cat: I Love My White Shoes by Eric Litwin

**Characters/Props:**

Pete the Cat

White Shoes

Red Shoes

Blue Shoes

Brown Shoes

**Setting:** Walking around town

**Props:** Cat puppet, Cut out pictures of the shoes in each color or real shoes

**Target Vocabulary:**

Brand new

White

Red

Blue

Brown

Pile

Goodness, no!

Bucket

Moral

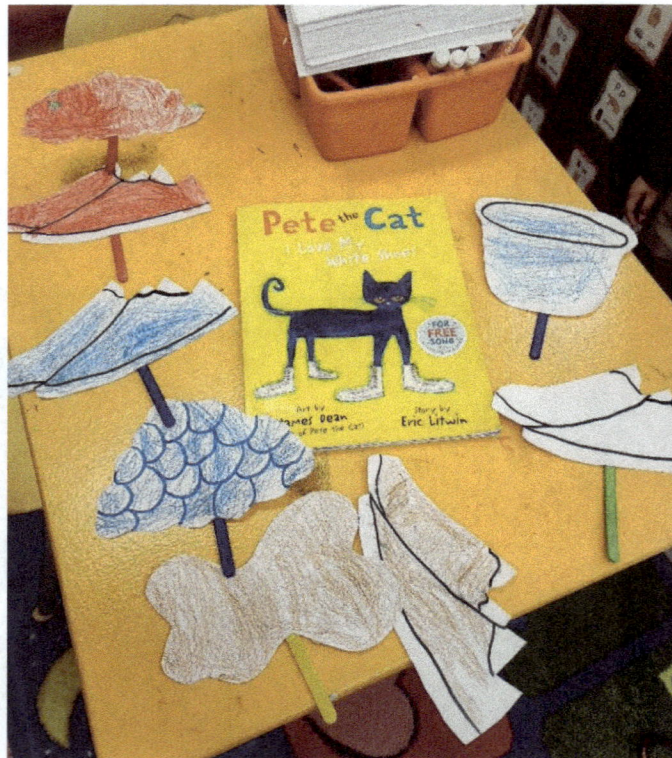

# There's An Alligator Under the Bed by Mercer Mayer

**Characters:**

Narrator                    Mom and Dad                    Alligator

**Setting:** Inside a house

**Suggested Props:** Plastic food, plastic alligator, bag, refrigerator from cardboard box

**Target Vocabulary:**

Alligator                   Up to me                       Crawled

Bait                        Followed                       Slammed

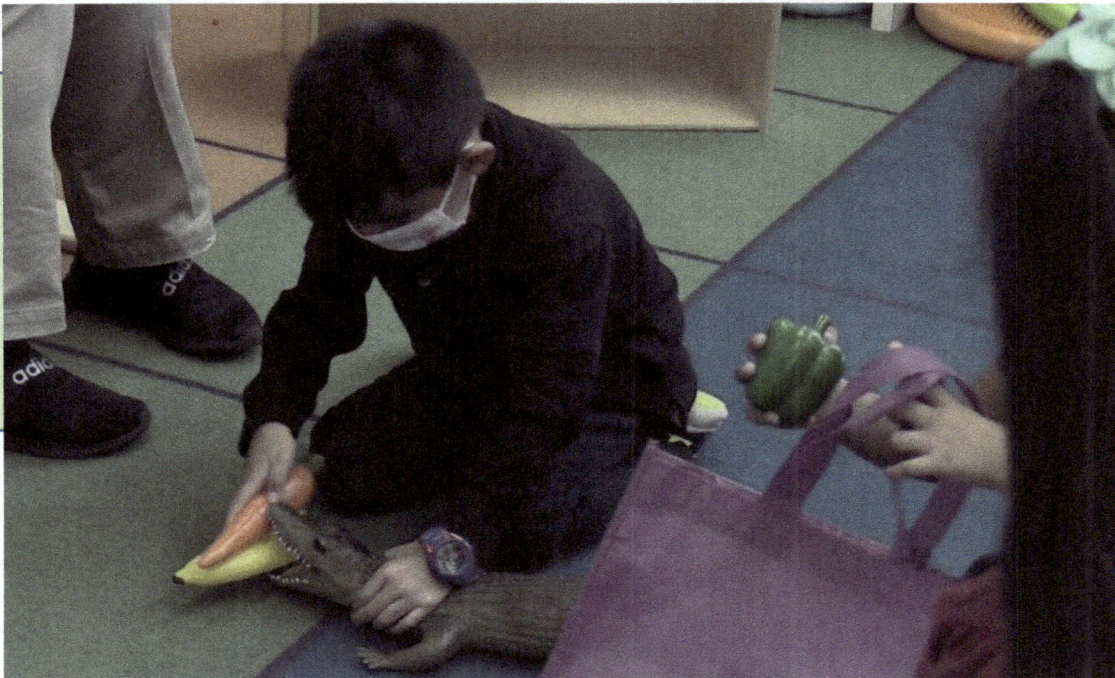

# Three Billy Goats Gruff – Traditional

**Characters:**

Big Billy Goat                    Small Billy Goat

Middle Billy Goat                 Troll

---

**Setting:** Meadow and River

**Suggested Props:** Puppets, small toys, headbands, or paper hats

---

**Target Vocabulary:**

Middle                    Meadow                    Troll

Valley                    Hideous

# The Three Little Pigs – Version by Bonnie Dobkin

**Characters:**

Mama Pig                    Three Pigs                    Wolf

**Setting:** Outside in the country; inside the pig's house

**Props:** Puppets or masks, hats, straw, sticks, bricks, big pot

**Target Vocabulary:**

Relaxed

Creative

Thoughtful

Advice

Skulking

Shady Grove

Logs

Trotted

Haystacks

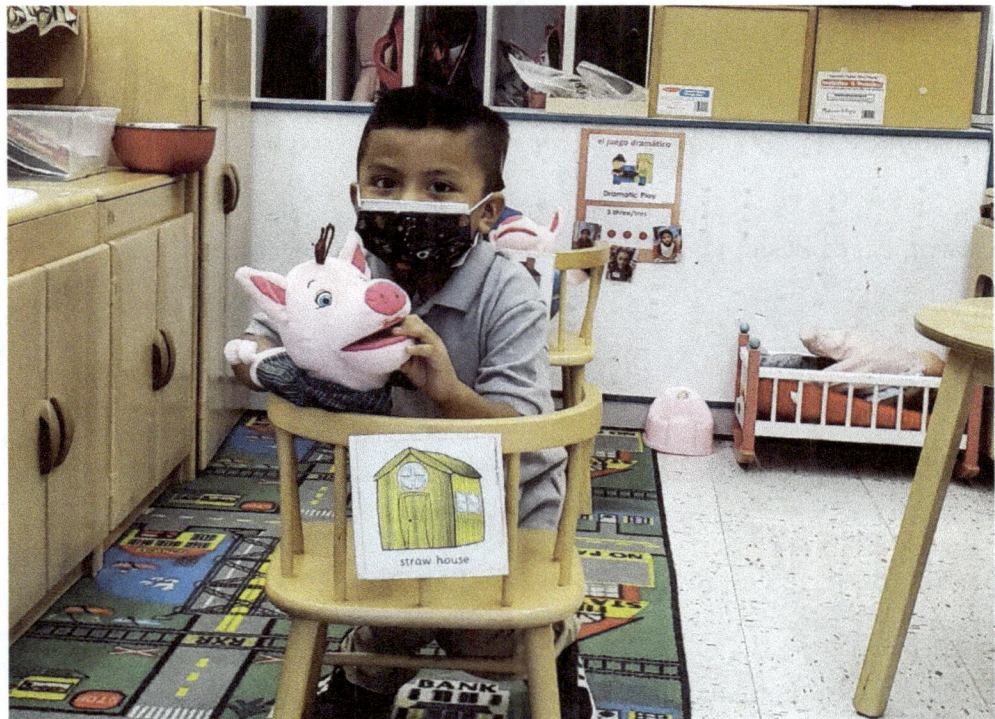

# Recommended Book List

Bentley, D. (2008). *The icky, sticky frog*. Atlanta: Piggy Toes Press.

Dobkin, B. (2010). *The three little pigs*. Bethesda, MD, Teaching Strategies.

Dobkin, B. (2010). *The Gingerbread Man*. Bethesda, MD, Teaching Strategies.

Carle, E. (1988). *The mixed-up chameleon*. New York: Harper Collins.

Carle, E. (1996). *The grouchy ladybug*. New York: Harper Collins.

Casanova, M. (2009). *One dog canoe*. New York: Square Fish.

Galdone, P. (2013). *Henny Penny*. Boston: Houghton Mifflin Harcourt.

Hutchins, P. (1989). *The doorbell rang*. New York: Greenwillow Books.

Litwin, E., & Dean, J. (2010). *Pete the cat: I love my white shoes*. New York: Harper.

Litwin, E. & Dean, J. (2012). *Pete the cat and his four groovy buttons*. New York: Harper.

Marshall, J. (1998). *Goldilocks and the three bears*. London: Puffin Books.

Martin, B., Jr. (1996) *Brown bear, brown bear*. New York: Holt.

Martin, B., Jr. & Archambault, J. (2000). *Chicka chicka boom boom*. San Diego, CA: Beach Lane Books.

Matsumoto, L. (2006). *A tale of two turtles: Adventures of Gary and Harry*. Honolulu, HI: Lehua.

Mayer, M. (1987). *There's an alligator under my bed*. New York: Penguin.

Ho, M. (2000). *Hush! A Thai lullaby*. New York: Scholastic.

Munsch, R. (2020). *The paper bag princess* (40th Anniversary Edition). Toronto: Annick Press.

Pinkney, J. (2017). *The three Billy goats gruff*. New York: Little Brown and Company.

Seeger, P. (1994). *Abiyoyo*. New York: Aladdin.

Wood, D., & Wood, A. (2020). *The little mouse, the red ripe strawberry, and the big hungry bear*. New York: Clarion Books.

Story Play: Bringing Books to Life in the Classroom

# Appendix A: Story Play Printables

Original drawings by Inkley @user10320847

**The Three Little Pigs**
Character: Big Bad Wolf

Story Play: Bringing Books to Life in the Classroom

**Three Billy Goats Gruff**
Character: Troll

Story Play: Bringing Books to Life in the Classroom

# Appendix B:
# How We Do Story Play in Our Classroom

You can use the story on the next few pages to teach your students the procedures and rules for story play. Copy and print out the pages and staple them together like a book. Read this to the children as an introduction to story play. You can also use the story on a one-on-one basis to read to students who might have trouble self-regulating during story play. For example, you might have a conference with a student, or small group of students, to go over the procedures. Read the story on the following pages and ask them to model how to behave. Practice carrying out a small story play session and give the students positive feedback when they are able to demonstrate appropriate behaviors.

# How We Do Story Play in Our Classroom

Sometimes in our classroom we read a story and then we act it out.

The teacher helps us choose characters in the story to act out.

Sometimes I have to wait for a turn to be a character. When I am waiting, I can be the audience.

The audience sits still, watches, and listens to the play. We clap at the end. Sometimes it's hard to wait, but I know I will get a turn.

When it's my turn to be a character, I hold the props very carefully.

I say the words from the book to act like the character. I also move like the character.

I listen to the other characters when they talk and move.

Story Play: Bringing Books to Life in the Classroom

When story time is over, the teacher puts the props in the library center. We can play with them by ourselves and act out the story.

It's a lot of fun to act out a story. I'm glad we do story play!

Story Play: Bringing Books to Life in the Classroom

# References

Cervetti, G. N., Pearson, P. D., Palincsar, A. S., Afflerbach, P., Kendeou, P., Biancarosa, G., ... & Berman, A. I. (2020). How the reading for understanding initiative's research complicates the simple view of reading invoked in the science of reading. *Reading Research Quarterly*, *55*, S161-S172.

Dickinson, D. K., Collins, M. F., Nesbitt, K., Toub, T. S., Hassinger-Das, B., Hadley, E. B., ... & Golinkoff, R. M. (2019). Effects of teacher-delivered book reading and play on vocabulary learning and self-regulation among low-income preschool children. *Journal of Cognition and Development*, *20*(2), 136-164.

Dickinson, D. K., Nesbitt, K. T., Collins, M. F., Hadley, E. B., Newman, K., Rivera, B. L., ... & Hirsh-Pasek, K. (2019). Teaching for breadth and depth of vocabulary knowledge: Learning from explicit and implicit instruction and the storybook texts. *Early Childhood Research Quarterly*, *47*, 341-356.

Hadley, E. B., & Dickinson, D. K. (2019). Cues for word-learning during shared book-reading and guided play in preschool. *Journal of Child Language*, *46*(6), 1202-1227.

Nicolopoulou, A., Cortina, K. S., Ilgaz, H., Cates, C. B., & de Sá, A. B. (2015). Using a narrative- and play-based activity to promote low-income preschoolers' oral language, emergent literacy, and social competence. *Early Childhood Research Quarterly*, *31*, 147-162.

Paley, V.G. (1981) *Wally's stories: Conversations in the kindergarten.* Cambridge, MA: Harvard University Press.

Paley, V.G. (1990) *The boy who would be a helicopter: The uses of storytelling in the classroom.* Cambridge, MA: Harvard University Press.

Paley, V.G. (1992) *You can't say you can't play.* Cambridge, MA: Harvard University Press.

Paley, V.G. (1997) *The girl with the brown crayon.* Cambridge, MA: Harvard University Press.

Rand, M. K., & Morrow, L. M. (2021). The contribution of play experiences in early literacy: expanding the science of reading. *Reading Research Quarterly, 56,* S239-S248.

Toub, T. S., Hassinger-Das, B., Nesbitt, K. T., Ilgaz, H., Weisberg, D. S., Hirsh-Pasek, K., ... & Dickinson, D. K. (2018). The language of play: Developing preschool vocabulary through play following shared book-reading. *Early Childhood Research Quarterly, 45,* 1-17.

Zosh, J. M., Hirsh-Pasek, K., Hopkins, E. J., Jensen, H., Liu, C., Neale, D., Solis, S. L., & Whitebread, D. (2018). Accessing the inaccessible: Redefining play as a spectrum. *Frontiers in Psychology, 9,* 1-12.

# About the Author

Muriel K. Rand is a professor of early childhood education at New Jersey City University. In addition to teaching at the college level, she is also a literacy coach, working with preschool and elementary teachers in New Jersey public schools. Dr. Rand has published a variety of books for early childhood teachers including: *The Positive Classroom field guide: Hands-on resources for creating a joyous elementary classroom*. Princeton Square Press (2015), *The Positive Classroom Method: 5 steps to a smooth-running classroom*. Princeton Square Press (2014), *The Positive Preschool: A Hands-on Guide for a Smooth-Running, Joyful Classroom*. Princeton Square Press (2014). *The Positive Classroom: Creating an Effective Learning Community for Young Children*. Princeton Square Press (2012). *Voices of Student Teachers: Cases from the Field* (Merrill, 2003), and *Giving it Some Thought: Cases for Early Childhood Practice* (NAEYC, 2000). She holds an Ed.D. and an M.S.W. degree from Rutgers University.

# About the Creative Designer

Catherine L. Rand is a free-lance artist and practicing elementary teacher. Her artwork and research center on literacy and creating equitable, research-based materials for classrooms. She also creates artwork for video games. Because games are fun.

www.ingramcontent.com/pod-product-compliance
Lightning Source LLC
LaVergne TN
LVHW061330060426

835513LV00015B/1344